Charles F. Bonser (Ed.)

Adapting Universities to the Global Society – A Transatlantic Perspective

AF185492

Transatlantic Public Policy Series

edited by

Eberhard Bohne

Professor of Public Administration
German University of Administrative Sciences Speyer and
German Research Institute for Public Administration

Charles F. Bonser

Dean Emeritus
Indiana University
School of Public and Environmental Affairs, Bloomington

Tony Bovaird

Professor of Public Management and Policy
University of Birmingham
School of Public Policy

Suzanne J. Piotrowski

Assistant Professor of Public Affairs and Administration
Rutgers University-Newark
School of Public Affairs and Administration

Volume 4

LIT

Adapting Universities
to the Global Society –
A Transatlantic Perspective

edited by

Charles F. Bonser

LIT

Bibliographic information published by the Deutsche Nationalbibliothek
The Deutsche Nationalbibliothek lists this publication in the Deutsche
Nationalbibliografie; detailed bibliographic data are available in the Internet at
http://dnb.d-nb.de.

ISBN 978-3-8258-1925-5

A catalogue record for this book is available from the British Library

® LIT VERLAG Dr. W. Hopf Berlin 2009

Fresnostr. 2 D-48159 Münster
Tel. +49 (0) 2 51-620 32 22 Fax +49 (0) 2 51-922 60 99
e-Mail: lit@lit-verlag.de http://www.lit-verlag.de

Distribution:

In Germany: LIT Verlag Fresnostr. 2, D-48159 Münster
Tel. +49 (0) 2 51-620 32 22, Fax +49 (0) 2 51-922 60 99, e-Mail: vertrieb@lit-verlag.de

In Austria: Medienlogistik Pichler-ÖBZ GmbH & Co KG
IZ-NÖ, Süd, Straße 1, Objekt 34, A-2355 Wiener Neudorf
Tel. +43 (0) 22 36-63 53 52 90, Fax +43 (0) 22 36-63 53 52 43, e-Mail: mlo@medien-logistik.at

In Switzerland: B + M Buch- und Medienvertriebs AG
Hochstr. 357, CH-8200 Schaffhausen
Tel. +41 (0) 52-643 54 85, Fax +41 (0) 52-643 54 35, e-Mail: order@buch-medien.ch

Distributed in the UK by: Global Book Marketing, 99B Wallis Rd, London, E9 5LN
Phone: +44 (0) 20 8533 5800 – Fax: +44 (0) 1600 775 663
http://www.centralbooks.co.uk/html

Distributed in North America by:

Transaction Publishers
New Brunswick (U.S.A.) and London (U.K.)

Transaction Publishers
Rutgers University
35 Berrue Circle
Piscataway, NJ 08854

Phone: +1 (732) 445 - 2280
Fax: + 1 (732) 445 - 3138
for orders (U. S. only):
toll free (888) 999 - 6778
e-mail: orders@transactionpub.com

Acknowledgments

I would like to recognize the several individuals who made the colloquium discussed here, as well as this publication, possible. First, Betty Fiscus, Administrative Assistant in the IU School of Public and Environmental Affairs Institute for Development Strategies, performed her usual magic in making conferences like this seem easy. She also helped organize the articles in this volume and dealt with most of the authors as they completed their comments. Kevin Kaiser, my former graduate assistant, also performed yeoman's work on the conference. He assisted with all of the myriad tasks of a conference like this, and also taped and summarized discussions. He also helped with the editing of some of the papers. The IU Conferences and the staff of the Indiana Memorial Union were easy to work with, very helpful and handled all of our needs expeditiously and professionally.

I also wish to thank the School of Public and Environmental Affairs, West European Studies, Bonser Lecture Series, IU International Programs, and the Institute for Development Strategies for their financial support of the conference.

My TPC colleague and co- editor of the Transatlantic Public Policy Series (TPPS), Eberhard Bohne of the German University of Administrative Sciences Speyer and the German Research Institute for Public Administration was his usual efficient and precise administration. His assistant, Andrea Langlotz, carried the complex burden of putting this publication in the shape needed by our publisher. Wera Veith-Joncic adapted the many tables and figures of the contributions to the manuscript format. Without the three of them, this publication would not have seen the light of day.

Kenneth M. Spencer has been the third co-editor of TPPS for several years. He asked to be relieved from his responsibilities as co-editor. I wish to thank him warmly for his support and cooperation of the last years.

I am glad to announce as successors to the editorship Tony Bovaird (University of Birmingham) and Suzanne J. Piotrowski (Rutgers University – Newark).

Finally, I would like to thank all of our TPC and other colleagues who took time from their busy schedules and travelled afar to attend this colloquium. It was a fascinating and enjoyable gathering and I greatly appreciate all of their contributions to the intellectual discourse. Needless to say, however, I assume all errors of omission or commission in this volume.

Bloomington, Indiana
November 2008   *Charles F. Bonser*

Table of Contents

Universities and Wealth Creation in Economic Regions

The Changing Nature of Universities: Governance, Competitiveness and Impact

Ten years of the Transatlantic Policy Consortium

Eberhard Bohne

TPC history and achievements

The idea of founding the TPC was born 10 years ago at a conference in Paris jointly sponsored by the School of Public and Environmental Affairs (SPEA), Indiana University and the Ecole National d'Administration (ENA). The driving force behind this idea was Charles F. Bonser. He was chosen the first chairman of the TPC when it was formally founded in spring of 2000. Ever since he has undertaken great efforts to organize the annual conferences on both sides of the Atlantic, to recruit new member institutions, and to motivate all members to contribute to the work of the TPC. A visible TPC result are five books which contain the presentations at the various conferences. The last three books are part of the new TPC Transatlantic Public Policy Series.

The idea behind the TPC

What is the idea behind the TPC?

In a 2002 SPEA memo on the TPC concerns are expressed "about the drifting and even increasingly hostile relationships between the US and Europe". The memo states an "interest in building or renewing transatlantic ties between higher education and training institutions".

But why this interest of Americans in the building and renewing of transatlantic ties in the 21st century? After all, many political pundits – in particular those from the neo-conservative camp – tell the Americans that Europe is today only of marginal relevance to the US. The future belongs to the US relationships with China, India and other Asian countries. Obviously, the author of the memo feels that the US and Europe are losing something vital for their future if the transatlantic rift continued to deepen. But what would be the loss?

In 2004 at the Austin conference, there was a dispute over the role of Islam in international terrorism. Some partly attributed Islamic terrorism to the fact that the Muslim countries had historically never experienced anything like the age of enlightenment. In my view, it is debatable whether the absence of the politico-philosophical movement of enlightenment in the Islamic world is a major cause of terrorism. However, there is probably a consensus that the pervasiveness and political power of international terrorism would be considerably smaller if the values of enlightenment were accepted worldwide. In any event, the values of enlightenment are historically shared by the US and Europe. Today, these values are threatened by religious and political fundamentalism on both sides of the Atlantic.

Religious and political fundamentalism is not only manifested in physical threats. It comes in many, often subtle intellectual facets whose political consequences tend to be overlooked or downplayed. Let me give you a few examples.

Reason, tolerance and liberty in enlightenment

Central concepts of enlightenment are reason, tolerance and liberty.

The concept of reason or rationality means the emancipation of the individual from religious, philosophical or political authorities. For example, Immanuel Kant's encouragement "Dare to use your own mind" became a motto of enlightenment.[1] Rationality is based on logic and empirical experience which form the foundations of modern science. The concept of rationality excludes the questions of religion. This is not because these questions are irrelevant or unimportant but because they cannot be answered by logic and experience. They are a matter of personal faith and conviction.

This separation of reason and religion is a prerequisite for religious tolerance.

Finally, the use of your own mind requires political liberty as Kant stressed. Thus, the principles of reason, tolerance and liberty are inter-related and represent the essence of enlightenment.[2]

These principles are also the foundations of our universities whose adaptation to the global society is the general theme of our conference.

The Pope's criticism of the concept of reason

No lesser person than the German Pope Benedict XVI strongly criticized this concept of reason and its separation from religion in a lecture which he gave in 2006 at Regensburg University in Germany. His lecture drew worldwide attention and harsh criticism from the Islamic world because it contained a quote by a Byzantine emperor from the 14th century who called Mohammed evil and inhuman. But the emperor also said "… not acting reasonably is contrary to God's nature".[3] This phrase was the starting point for the Pope to elaborate on the relationship between reason and Christian faith. The message of his lecture culminated in a strong criticism of Western secularism.

The Pope holds that there is no separation between the Christian God and reason.[4] God is reason. As the Evangelist John says: "In the beginning was the logos and the logos is God." The Greek term "logos" means both reason and word. The Pope goes on: "… The Church has always insisted that between his [God's] eternal Creator Spirit and our created reason there exists a real analogy…". He considers the denial of this analogy a danger for man and particularly for the West.[5]

The question, however, is who determines the characteristics and scope of the analogy between reason and the Christian God? According to the Pope, it is the Church. Thus, reason is subjected to an authority.

Furthermore, if Christian faith and reason are linked together, other religions are necessarily unreasonable.

This convergence of reason and faith is anti-enlightenment, and the key characteristic of religious fundamentalism.[6] The Pope's praise of enlightenment and of the achievements of modern science does not refute this conclusion.

Political implications

The deadly consequences of Islamic political and religious fundamentalism are evident.

The Pope's subtle usurpation of rationality by religious doctrine expressed in the language of Hellenistic philosophy also has dangerous political consequences:

First, it provides the enemies of enlightenment with a theoretical underpinning for their attacks on rationality, religious tolerance and political liberty. There is a widespread sentiment in Europe and the US that the Christian culture has to be protected from the intrusion of irrational and godless peoples.

Second, the convergence between reason and faith is used by the Pope as a criterion of European identity.[7] This means in political terms that the Islamic Turkey is to be excluded from the European Union. I think one can raise practical objections to Turkey's accession to the EU. However, different religions and concepts of rationality should be irrelevant for this question. Otherwise one encourages the very "clash of civilizations" described by Huntington.[8]

Third, domestically almost all European countries are experiencing internal cultural clashes mainly due to the unresolved problems of integrating ethnic minorities:

- In Germany, no-go areas are emerging for dark people.
- In France, suburbs have burned.
- In the UK, bombs were planted in London.
- In the Netherlands, political assassination occurred.
- Denmark plunged into a deep crisis over anti-Islamic caricatures.
- In East European countries para-military groups and political parties are emerging which decry Western decadence and seek to protect – what they call – the true ethnic identity of Poles, Czechs or Hungarians.[9]

I think, Europe is in real trouble.

Fourth, I believe that the US are in real trouble, too. The political alliance between chauvinistic neo-conservatives and evangelical fundamentalists is, in my view, an attack on the principles of enlightenment and politically very dangerous. The disastrous consequences for US foreign relations are evident.

I think that domestic crises are ahead if the creationist movement is not contained. Evolutionary biology has throughout history been a key target for all enemies of enlightenment.[10]

Conclusions

The solutions to these problems cannot be expected from governments alone. It is essential that civil society organizes and defends the values of enlightenment. *This is, in my view, the idea behind the TPC.*

The TPC has become a forum for a rational, tolerant and free discourse between Americans and Europeans.

Endnotes

[1] See *Arno Baruzzi* 1968. Kant, in: *Hans Maier, Heinz Rausch und Horst Denzer*, Klassiker des politischen Denkens, München: C. H. Beck, pp. 161-186, 163.

[2] See: *Werner Schneiders* 2005. Vernunft und Freiheit, in: Philosophie der Aufklärung – Aufklärung der Philosophie, Gesammelte Studien edited by *Frank Grunert*, Berlin: Duncker & Humblot, pp. 207-223, 215.

[3] *Benedict XVI*, Faith, reason and the university. Memories and reflections, Regensburg, 20 September 2006. An English translation is accessible at <http://www.cwnews.com/news/viewstory.cfm?recnum=46474>, p. 2.

[4] See En. 3, p. 3; *Wolfgang Krebs* 2007. Das Papstzitat von Regensburg. Benedikt XVI im "Kampf der Kulturen", Berlin: Rhombos, p. 163.

[5] See *Krebs* (En. 4), p. 172.

[6] See *Krebs* (En. 4), p. 138.

[7] See En. 3, p. 3 f.

[8] *Samuel Huntington* 1996. The clash of civilizations, New York: Simon and Schuster.

[9] See: *Magdalena Marsovszky*, Die neue Gefahr in Osteuropa, Süddeutsche Zeitung, No. 196, 27 August 2007, p. 2.

[10] See *Krebs* (En. 4), p. 139.

1

Introduction

Charles F. Bonser

For 10 years the Transatlantic Policy Consortium (TPC) has explored a variety of policy issues of importance to both Europe and North America. A visit to our web site: <http://www.spea.indiana.edu/tac/> offers a review of the organization's goals, our previous work, and information on the membership. This volume is based on a colloquium, "Adapting Universities to a Global Society - A Transatlantic Perspective", that was held on the Bloomington Campus of Indiana University in September 2007. It is clear that this colloquium theme was very timely. Universities in both the United States and Europe are presently engaged in frame breaking discussions about how globalization is and will further affect their performance and mission, their overall role in society, and how they are or should evolve into new types of institutions to better serve the needs of their constituencies.

The colloquium divided itself into four key sets of presentations and discussions. Keynote overview comments were offered by Richard Legon, President of the U.S. Association of Governing Boards of Universities and Colleges; Manuel Heitor, Secretary of State for Science, Technology, and Higher Education of Portugal; and by Hans-Jürgen Blinn, Ministry of Education, Science, Youth, and Culture of Rhineland-Palatinate, Germany.

Key issues raised by Richard Legon include changing accountability, access to higher education, the impact of rapidly escalating costs, and in many states, the de-facto privatization of research oriented state universities.

Secretary Heitor offers extensive statistical analysis of the changing shape of Higher Education in Europe. Issues include the increasingly competitive nature of the higher education landscape globally, and responses by the institutions and the European Union. He discusses the large differences in societal engagement among the several European nations and the moves toward mergers or consortia as a way to deal with international competition. He compares the U.S. and the European universities and notes the significant differences in societal support, research, management autonomy, and in leadership strength. He suggests the gap in research and development between U.S. and European universities is increasing. The quality issues addressed in the on-going debate in Europe initiated in 1999 by the "Bologna Process" are also introduced.

Hans-Jürgen Blinn first focuses on the regional dimension of higher education in Europe, utilizing the German Länder (states) as an example. Issues include coordination between the federal and regional entities and he contrasts these in some cases to the U.S. states and the national government. Blinn also argues that the "European Higher Education Area is situated at the crossroads of research, education, and innovation", and the EU, through the European Council, has set the objective of making the European education and training system a "world quality reference" by 2010. He then explores progress in meeting this objective, and associated initiatives, issues and problems arising from the nature of the international market – estimated at $30 billion per year – for educational services.

The discussion that followed these presentations centered on four key themes:
- The relationship between states and universities, and the amount that universities are state controlled or controlled by other societal influences
- Fragmentation vs. Standardization: To what extent and at what level should universities be organized: on a country level, university level, program level?
- Higher education for the few or many: Educate the best and the brightest or offer it for many people?

- Cross cultural education: While universities are beginning to go global, they are also going very local

The second set of presentations focuses on the "University Quality Challenge".

Siegfried Magiera (University of Speyer) as well as Frans-Bauke van der Meer and Arthur Ringeling present two different approaches to achieving quality education in the professions, including the integration of work practice in professional education: one, the German system of public administration professional education; the other, public administration education for the part time professional student in the same field in The Netherlands.

Laure Castin (University of Reims), offers a case example of the implementation of the Bologna Process, referred to earlier, in France. She reminds us that: "The main idea was to create an open space where students, graduates, and higher education staff could benefit from unhampered mobility and equitable access to high quality higher education through mutual recognition of any degrees, transparency (readable and comparable degrees organized in a three-cycle-structure) and cooperation in quality assurance."

However, one of the several paradoxes of Bologna, for example, is that its underlying values – solidarity, equal opportunities, partnerships, etc. - are in conflict with the global competitive context in which our universities find themselves. She goes on to discuss how France is facing these paradoxes and the conflicts, governmental initiatives, and debates that accompany this effort. In her view, "Equality policy is over. To cope with that requires a totally new university culture and state of mind in France."

The third section of this report focuses on universities and their impact on wealth creation in economic regions. David Audretsch (Indiana University and the Max Planck Institute of Economics) examines both the traditional role of universities in economic development, and what has been the impact of globalization on universities. He then explains how and why globalization "rendered the public policy framework ineffective, and how a new framework, based on entrepreneurship, is replacing it." Finally, he examines how the role of the university is evolving in the "entrepreneurial society."

In the second contribution in this group, Alan Rugman (Indiana University) looks at globalization and higher education in a regional context. He believes that a more sophisticated view of globalization is that most firms have expanded their trade and foreign investment mainly on an intra-regional basis. This, he argues, has special implications for higher education. He thinks there is a danger that such faulty analyses of globalization as one finds in the popular literature (e.g., "The World is Flat") will drive university policy. Instead he argues for a regional, rather than global, higher education competitive paradigm.

The final four contributions of this report are concerned with the changing nature of university governance. Michael Kelly (Higher Education Authority of Ireland) discusses academic policy, autonomy, and government regulation of higher education. He notes that: "The last decade has seen a huge shift in attitude on both sides of the Atlantic in relation to the constructive role of strong corporate governance in higher education." There are several reasons for this shift, including the governance failures that have caused significant problems in private sector organizations. He discusses several implications of this shift, and offers guidance to achieve goals of good governance.

Jeffrey Hart (Indiana University) discusses organizational cultures and internal organization in U.S. research oriented universities. He focuses on two models: one applies mainly to the natural and social sciences, and is characterized by governmental funding of research. The other is used primarily in non scientific units. The former, in his view, affects tenure and promotion decisions and university governance by rewarding faculty who publish in peer reviewed outlets; the other pushes faculty in the direction of balancing research, teaching, and service.

Chancellor Ken Gros Louis (Indiana University) recognizes that significant world-wide changes are being reshaped by scientific and technological innovations, global interdependence, cross-cultural encounters, and changes in the balance of economic and political power. These shifts are dramatically impacting higher education. He presents an international strategy for American universities that is based on:

- Education and Service Learning Abroad;
- Global Institutional Engagement;
- Global Faculty Research; and
- International Outreach and Service.

He argues that these must be accomplished while maintaining our core values as public universities and with a responsibility to the welfare of the citizens of the state.

In the final contribution, Arthur Hauptman (Washington, D.C.) presents four challenges now faced by higher education policy makers around the world. These are: 1) matching resources to keep up with rapidly growing demand for higher education; 2) improving equity throughout the educational pipeline; 3) increasing the external efficiency of the system; and 4) raising internal efficiency of the tertiary system by improving productivity. He then proposes several ways in which these issues can be confronted.

Issues of Higher Education
in Europe

2

The European Research Universities and the Challenge for Science and Technology in Europe

Manuel Heitor

The debate on the emerging reform of European Universities is considered in terms of the allocation and future evolution of R&D expenditure in Europe, which must consider the different nature of private and public incentives for science and technology (S&T) and foster the strategic collaborative involvement of both public and private stakeholders. "Blanket" recommendations to enhance property rights or to limit public resource allocation, based on perceptions of the US experience, may be misguided. In fact, the key message that emerges from analyzing the US patterns of investment in S&T over the long-run is that the development of the US S&T system was based on a diversity of policies that led over time to increased opportunities for citizens, as well as to increased "institutional specialization" based on a clear separation of the role of private and public incentives to support S&T.

How far will Europe be able to strengthen a public funding policy for R&D that is oriented, focused, and consistent? This is particularly relevant when compared with the US experience, where public funding has been relatively focused and consistently oriented towards academic and basic research. Europe, in contrast, has had a public funding policy that is diffuse and non-focused, attempting to fulfil a number of different objectives, and varying over time to accommodate circumstantial and shifting priorities leading to inconsistent allocations over time. The recent successful launching of the European Research Council provides a new orientation and suggests that Europe needs to increase public funding of R&D and that this public funding should be consistently allocated and oriented towards academic and basic research in a way that can foster the knowledge infrastructure. Fostering and maintaining the excellence of this knowledge infrastructure is the most effective way for public funding of R&D to be able to provide new opportunities for all citizens and facilitate the necessary resources (including qualified human skills) for firms to increase their own investment in science and technology, as well as to promote the entrepreneurial environment necessary to innovation.

Introduction

Over the course of ten years between the mid-1990s to the mid-2000s, the total number of student enrollment in higher education institutions worldwide nearly doubled. As a result, institutions are engaging in and moving towards new kinds of transnational partnerships and mergers.[1] But in comparison to the United States, European universities must overcome a greater number of challenges in this competitive and global educational landscape. For instance, large differences exist between Europe and the United States in the type of student engaged in higher education learning and the level of performance of individual universities. European universities not only have a smaller ratio of students between the ages of 20 and 29 enrolled in tertiary education compared to the United States, but the United States has significantly more universities ranked highly by the leading university ranking references. Additionally, differences in the strength of institutional leadership, suggested by significantly fewer highly cited researchers at European institutions, and autonomy separate European and American universities.[2]

Perhaps most importantly, Europe faces a critical challenge in fostering research and development (R&D) in society and promoting research training at the university level. This challenge also includes understanding how to learn and teach in research universities. Identifying and learning the best modes of teaching, strategies, and practices at research universities could take many years, but even these best practices may not prove to be effective and efficient across all universities. Additionally, a need to strengthen strategies for science culture throughout society and to recruit students willing to undertake research activities at European universities pose as obstacles to generating more human resources for science, engineering, and technology in Europe.[3] There is a perception of science education in schools as an abstract area of study due to a general lack of opportunities to engage in experimental and observational research. Perhaps opening research laboratories and industries to undergraduate students may cultivate a growing interest in science and technology oriented careers and contribute to the development of more scientists in European society.[4]

This Colloquium on "Adapting Universities to the Global Society" was organized for good reasons: in benefit of people, knowledge and ideas, as well as in recognition of the increased role universities play in modern societies. The ultimate goal is to look at goals and challenges to be achieved through diversified national policies and institutional strategies.

This is because higher education systems are under pressure to meet demands imposed by a globalised knowledge-society without compromising quality deliverance. Although most European institutions and their staff have recognized the need for change for many years, the way institutions are organized, either internally, or through traditional links with society, as well as their structure of incentives, have continuously delayed reforms. Consequently, it is only in recent years that reforms have emerged directly conducted by governments in many different countries and political regimes. The Portuguese system is no exception to these mounting pressures and change has been recently introduced through governmental actions.

In particular, it has been questioned how to attract and sustain new talents in Europe and how universities can meet the global challenges of research and international competition for highly qualified human resources? In a context of increased "brain circulation" throughout the world, how far public funding for research in EU, including that provided through the EU Framework Programme, can accommodate funding of post-graduate education and the building-up of well recognized graduate schools? This is particularly relevant because funding of academic and basic R&D in EU should be consistent with that of post-graduate education, notably through joint master and doctorate programs organized on the bases of graduate schools with an international scope. In addition, graduate programs across disciplines should be able to provide the supply of adequate transferable skills to allow for a highly skilled labour force that is able to create and drive new markets. This will increase the competitiveness of European research universities and better educate and qualify highly skilled personnel. It will also play a fundamental role in promoting leading edge research activities and to increase the relevance of Europe in attracting talents in the emergent pattern of globalized brain circulation.

This paper addresses these questions from two different, but interrelated perspectives, namely the funding mechanisms and the need to promote dynamic and responsive universities, including the need to foster their internationalisation.

Reforming funding systems

Figure 1 shows that EU15 has doubled its gross expenditure in R&D, GERD, over the last 25 years, but the gap on the gross expenditure on R&D between US and EU has increased, with the gross American expenditure in R&D increased by more than 2.3 times over the same period. At the same time, China has increased its GERD by more than 5 times in the last decade.

The strong economic performance of the U.S. economy over the 1990s, along with the changes outlined above, has contributed to a general and widespread shift towards market-based, rather than publicly supported, incentives for science and technology in most OECD countries, and, especially, in Europe. In fact, the conclusions of the European Union intergovernmental summit held in Lisbon in 2000 (i.e., the so-called "Lisbon Summit"[5]) can be interpreted as a call for Europe to enact policies that, in part, seek to replicate and improve upon the innovation-based economic performance that has characterized the U.S. economic growth. But, overall, private spending on R&D in EU15 has remained stable since 2000 at around 80 billion and has not followed the related American increase during the 90′s, as documented in Figure 2. In addition, public spending in Europe has just slightly increased.

Figure 1. Gross Expenditure on R&D in EU15, US, China and sample industrialized countries

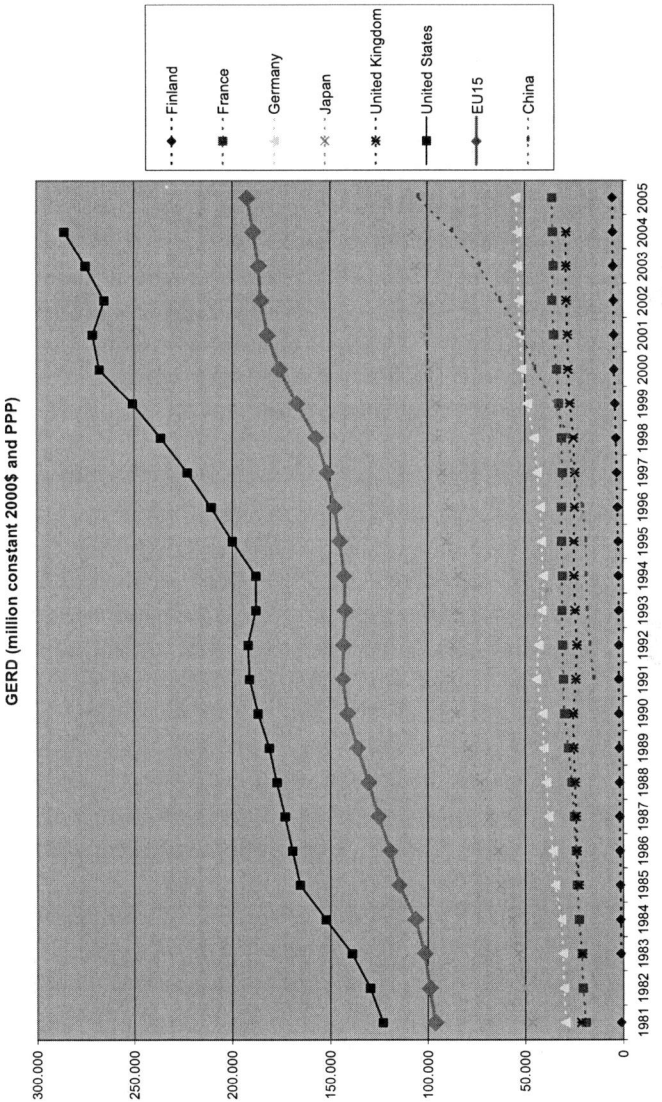

Figure 2. Private and Public Spending on R&D in EU15 and in the United States

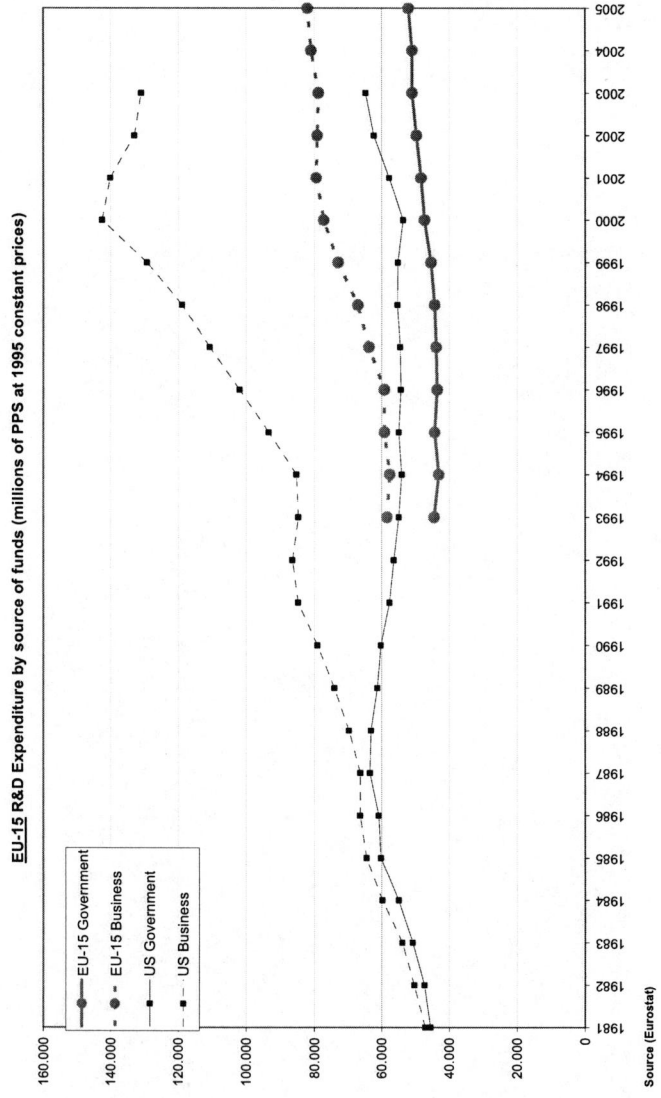

An examination of the sources of funding and amount of expenditures towards R&D in Europe and the United States offers some insight in to the reasons for the challenges discussed above. The ratio of public expenditure compared to industry expenditure on R&D in Europe is low, but there has been a long and persistent downward trend in this ratio in both the EU and the United States. Despite the growth in the amount of funding from private sources in the United States, public expenditure towards basic R&D has not gone away. Instead, it has increased since the mid-1990s and continues to push upwards private spending on basic R&D.

Figure 3 complements the analysis first published by Conceição et al. (2004)[6] for the US and compares the ratio of public vs. private expenditure of the total expenditure (vertical axis) and the ratio only for basic expenditure (horizontal axis) since the post-war period until 2006. It is possible to identify four stages in Figure 3. First, the growth of total public funding overall through 1965, when public expenditure was two times as much as private expenditure. Throughout this period, the ratio in basic expenditure remains relatively stable at around 2, increasing to 2.5 at the peak of total public/private expenditure. This is the "launch" period of the U.S. S&T system. Then, from 1966 through 1987, the total public/private ratio decreased rapidly but, at the same time, the basic R&D public/private ratio increased rapidly. This is the "1st specialization" period, as the U.S. public funding focuses more on basic R&D, as applied research and development is left increasingly to the private sector. Third, through the 1990s, the trend is that both ratios are decreasing, although the basic science one is still very high, around 3. Finally, and surprisingly enough, since 2000 we observe a "2nd specialization" period, as the U.S. public funding focuses again more on basic R&D, with the private sector also increasing its funding of basic research, although at relatively moderate levels.

Following the analysis of Conceição et al. (2004) it is noted that another important aspect revealed by the "structural analysis" mentioned above is that much of the retreat in public funding in the United States is related with the pulling back of financial support to defense-related R&D. In fact, for the first time since 1980, the non-defense related R&D public expenditure in the United States is equal to the defense related expenditure. It is also important to note that the abrupt decrease in public expenditure of 1987 is related to the start of the decrease of the defense-related expenditure. The non-defense public expenditure on R&D in the United States has been on an increasing trend for more than 20 years.

The growth in non-defense public R&D expenditure in the US has been going mostly to health and to basic science. In 1999 the U.S. Congress committed itself to double the funding of the National Institutes of Health (which funds research in health-related areas) and of the National Science Foundation (which funds basic science). Preliminary budget requests of the Bush administration for 2003 comply with this commitment, putting the funding of the National Institutes of Health at close to US$ 30 billion. But the analysis of Conceição et al. (2004) has also shown that the public allocation of R&D resources to universities has exhibited a persistent increasing trend over the last half century. While historically federal labs and private industry have received most of the federal funds (private industry with two great peaks by the mid 1960s and by the mid 1980s), if current trends continue universities will be the main receivers of public support to R&D in the United States.

Enhancing the level of public expenditures in the EU to improve the science and technology environment in Europe has several policy implications. First, the debate related to increasing expenditure in R&D in Europe needs to improve the understanding of the different nature of private and public incentives for science and technology. For instance, creating "blanket" recommendations to enhance property rights or to limit public resource allocation may be misguided. Looking at the US experience shows that a diversity of policies and increasing "institutional specialization," in addition to the clarification of the role of the private and public incentives to support science and technology, is needed when making R&D policy. Increasing and strengthening public funding for R&D also requires orienting funding towards academic and basic research in a way that will foster the knowledge infrastructure, offering funding that will provide companies with the necessary resources to increase their own investment in science and technology, and allowing funding to foster the entrepreneurial environment and facilitate new entries in the market.[7]

Figure 3. Ratio of Public to Private Expenditure for Total R&D and for Basic R&D in the United States

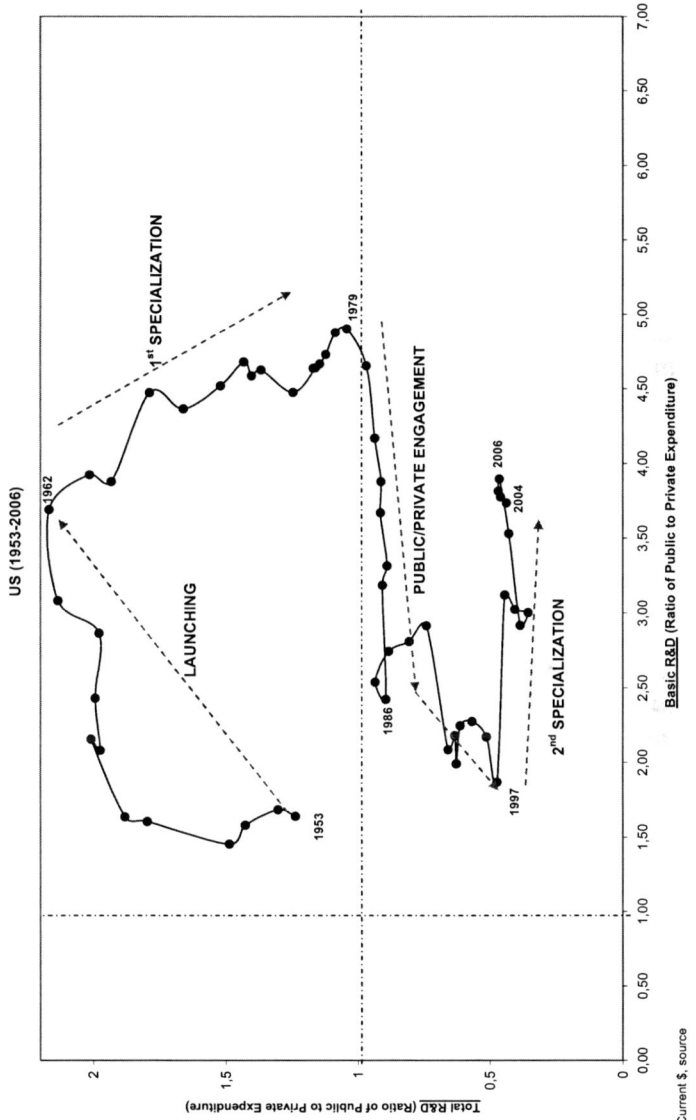

In fact, analysis shows that the need to modernise funding mechanisms, and ensure a better balance between institutional and competitive funding for universities, has become a key issue to meet the global challenges of research and international competition. This certainly includes the need to preserve the institutional integrity of the university,[8] as well as to create flexible financial mechanisms to attract and secure new talents in Europe. But it may also require, as shown by Paul David and Sten Metcalfe, increased competition and collaborative patterns among funding agencies in Europe.[9] We need to strengthen the role of the European Research Council and to foster additional competitive funding schemes with a transnational configuration by promoting collaborative arrangements among national funding agencies in Europe.

In this regard, and following the emerging discussion in Europe about the future of science and technology,[10] it is clear that, by and large, the financing of higher education and of science and innovation has occurred in Europe along rather traditional lines. Governments directly undertake R&D or subsidize (directly or indirectly, through tax measures) R&D performance and technological innovation. Governments rise – or forego – revenue to pay for this support. Yet, the history of science is rich with varied means of financing science and technological innovation. More importantly, developments in the size, integration, and technologies available in global capital markets present the opportunity to think about new financing possibilities. These involve both the channeling of resources from the global liquidity pools to science and technology, as well as enhanced risk management tools that are as important aspects of "financing" as channeling money.

Promoting dynamic and responsive universities

The analysis above calls for the relevance and opportunity of the emerging modernizing agenda for higher education in Europe and, in particular, of research universities. But, again, reference terms require clarification, namely in terms of the perception built in many European constituencies about the reality of American universities regarding knowledge production and diffusion. Many authors over the last two decades[11] argue that whatever does not harm the institutional integrity of the university is acceptable. Companies and universities have evolved in a social context, to the point of attaining what these authors call "institutional speciality". Thus, whereas companies are concerned to obtain private returns for the knowledge that they generate, universities have traditionally made it public. By means of this specialisation, or "division of labour", the accumulation of knowledge has taken place at a rapid pace, as is shown by the unprecedented levels of economic growth since the end of the Second World War.

This argument can be analyzed in detail, in the context of the knowledge-based economies.[12] The threats to a university's institutional integrity in fact go beyond the extension of its activities to links with society, which, if excessive, could lead to resources being spread too thinly. This analysis is based on the more serious problems that may arise if higher education institutions take the path of privatising the ideas that they produce and the skills that they develop.

We may begin by analyzing the higher education function of teaching, which contributes to the accumulation of knowledge, specifically of skills, through the formal process of learning through education, or "learning by learning". This process is divergent:[13] a university education combines the transmission of codified knowledge by the teachers with the individual characteristics of the students, in a process in which the interpretation of ideas leads to the accumulation of unique skills. Given this situation, each student can profit from these skills in the future. The university may therefore be tempted to increase the direct tuition to the students, as a way of increasing its income.

Besides the well-known externalities associated with higher education, which justify state support for education in virtually every country in the world with the possible exception of Japan, analysis of the need to provide the skills necessary for the information society in which we live strengthens the arguments in favour of state support for higher education. The threat of increased privatisation of teaching skills could thus cause serious problems, in that it would lead to a reduction in the resource that really is in short supply in the knowledge-based economies: the skills to use and interpret ideas. This conclusion does not cast doubt on the contributions currently made by students, but rather questions a possible trend that could jeopardise the institutional integrity of the university itself, if the tendency to decrease public funding persists.

Moving on to research, it is worth noting that the great majority of the ideas that are generated in universities are of a public nature, this being the essence of the specific contribution that the university makes to the accumulation of ideas. Incentives for the production of these public ideas come from a complex system of reward and prestige within the academic community. In a well known survey of university teachers in the late nineties in the United States, the most satisfying factor, chosen by 86.2 % of the sample, was autonomy and independence.[14] Again, the temptation to privatize university research results could threaten fundamental aspects of the way universities work and their essential contribution to the accumulation of ideas.

To summarise, our conclusion is that the institutional integrity of the university should be preserved, and an important point in terms of public policy is that state funding of universities should not be reduced. However, this measure by itself is not enough. From a more pragmatic viewpoint, the university should respond to the needs of society, which include rapid and unforeseeable changes in the structure of the employment market and the need to furnish its graduates with new skills beyond purely technical ones, in particular learning skills. The need to promote dynamic and responsive universities considers widening the scope of diversity and of institutional autonomy, while ensuring effective accountability. Again, and always, it must encompass preserving the institutional integrity of the university, at the same time new forms of knowledge production (namely in the way presented since the early 90's by Gibbons and colleagues)[15] should be considered in reforming the university and its links with society.

We have seen, especially in Continental Europe, that raising the level of autonomy for higher education institutions (HEIs) is one of the main objectives of sector reforms across different countries in recent years. Granting independent legal status to HEIs is one means of achieving this goal: it gives HEIs greater autonomy to govern themselves and function as they see most appropriate, in a free and independent way, in pursuit of work that is deemed essential to society.[16]

The global landscape, the challenges facing higher education in Europe, and low levels of public expenditures on R&D underscore the need to engage in further higher education reforms within Europe, to address the science and technology challenges, particularly in the context of the ongoing Bologna process. So far, reform efforts do appear to be leading to some successes. Even though the Bologna process is voluntary, most institutions recognize the great challenges and opportunities facing higher education in Europe and have been making efforts to incorporate Bologna issues into their specific institutional strategies and activities. Furthermore, most institutions view the Bologna process as an opportunity to address many of the problems that have long existed in Europe. There are, however, challenges that still remain in this reform movement to adapt higher education in Europe to the global landscape and to improve funding for R&D. Understanding the relationship between Bologna reforms and the social and national contexts in which they take place and expanding the European policy dialogue in higher education to include more issues, remain significant challenges in the current process.

Within this debate, the need to foster the internationalization of universities is emerging, either in terms of promoting student mobility or, above all, European university networks able to foster attractive and competitive research and learning environments and to attract and train highly qualified human resources. The key issue is the creation of international partnerships able to strengthen institutions and the necessary critical masses to compete at the highest international level and, at the same time, guarantee the adequate level of institutional integrity of the university.

In addition, recognizing scientific knowledge as a "public good" introduces the need to consider new policy dimensions in science and technology policy that are designed and implemented in a way that fosters independent scientific institutions, among which the way in which transnational institutions are organized may provide a useful framework.

We know that casual observations have shown that patterns of scientific strength and weakness are strongly influenced by the nature of the societal and technological problems to be solved. In any case, current understanding of the complexities of the knowledge base that underlie future scientific and technological advancement is very limited, and this led Keith Pavitt to conclude many years ago that "the aim of policy should be to create a broad and productive science base, closely linked to higher (and particularly post-graduate) education, and looking outward both to applications and to developments in other parts of the world."[17]

It is also in this context that major efforts have been undertaken to promote the internationalization of the Portuguese scientific community. In particular, a strategic program of international partnerships in science, technology and higher education was initiated in 2006 and by September 2007 the first doctoral and advanced studies program were officially launched, bringing together several Portuguese universities and leading universities worldwide, including, MIT, Carnegie Mellon University and the University of Texas at Austin. Unprecedented in Portugal, these programmes facilitated the creation in 2007 of effective thematic networks involving a large set of Portuguese institutions with the objective of stimulating their internationalisation through advanced studies projects and sustainable schemes to stimulate new knowledge and exploit new ideas in collaboration with companies and internationally renowned institutions, as follows:

– The MIT-Portugal Programme,[18] launched on 11 October 2006 in the field of "engineering systems", attributing special emphasis to the complex processes associated with industrial production systems, sustainable energy systems, bio-engineering systems and transport systems, in which Portuguese and MIT faculty and researchers identified over 30 priority areas for research and development in close cooperation with an industrial affiliation programme.

– The CMU-Portugal Programme,[19] was also launched in October 2006, but with emphasis on information and communication technologies and involving dual professional masters and PhD programmes by Portuguese institutions and Carnegie Mellon University (namely in Software Engineering, Information Networking, Information Security, Human Computer Interaction, entrepreneurship and technological Change, Mathematics and Language Technology.

– Under the University of Texas in Austin - Portugal Programme, launched in March 2007,[20] the following areas were selected: i) digital content and multimedia production and distribution; ii) advanced computing; and iii) science and technology commercialization, including establishing a "university technology enterprise network".

Higher education institutes play an important role in improving the science and technology society in Europe, and policy needs to address this role. Graduate programs and schools with a strong international component need to be able to provide the supply of adequate transferable skills to allow for a highly skilled labor force that is able to create and drive new markets. Strengthening higher education institutions, particularly through strengthening institutional autonomy and regulatory regimes, can also serve as a way to overcoming the science and technology challenges in Europe. Greater autonomy may improve the responsiveness of institutions to an expanded set of national and societal demands. Strengthening regulatory regimes may also serve this goal and lead to an overall higher education sector that is more autonomous, too.

Summary

If any conclusion can be taken from the discussion above, is that there is a consensus about the need, and the opportunity, to accelerate reform of European universities in order not only to stimulate progress across the whole higher education system, but also to foster the emergence and strengthening of European higher education institutions which can demonstrate their excellence at international level. In our current socio-economic context, Europe's universities aim to become worldwide competitive players, particularly in research. We certainly need new approaches to research & education in environments of increased global competition for talent.

But accelerating reform requires the need to concentrate higher education reform on a myriad of issues that will ultimately open the "Black Box" associated with all type of higher education institutions, preserving autonomy while building-up a new set of relationships with society at large and introducing an "intelligent accountability" associated with a renewed structure of incentives. And this must be achieved in a way that will promote new leaderships for Europe's universities.

This, *per si*, may require promoting a European market of excellence for university leaders, as also a critical path to attract our best researchers to take the lead of our universities.[21]

I would also argue that strengthening external university links such as public and private research organisations and vocational training institutions, are critical in making the institutional changes required to meet the needs of global competition and the knowledge economy.

By focusing governmental and political actions on the external dimension, higher education institutions are asked to strengthen their capacity to make the critical internal changes for modernising their systems of teaching and research within a path of diversity and specialisation, without compromising quality. Furthermore, by enhancing their external links with society, higher education institutions are asked to carefully improve their relationships with economic, social and political actors, thereby creating "new" reinforced institutions that have gained societal trust.

In this respect, and following some of the issues raised by John Ziman[22] many years ago and also noted by Nobel Laureate Richard Ernst (2003),[23] one critically important and emerging institutional issue refers to the training of students and young scientists in order to provide them with core competencies that help them to become successful researchers and prepare them with the adequate "transferable skills" for the job market outside research and academia.

To cope with such a variety of demands and with a continuously changing environment, we all know that the higher education system, in particular, needs to be diversified. But the challenge of establishing common European goals and diversified national policies towards the "modernization of European universities" requires effective university networks and a platform of research universities, notably for stimulating the political debate among the various stakeholders and for assisting in the networking of national constituencies promoting the positioning of Europe in the emerging paths of brain circulation worldwide.

Endnotes

[1] P. Conceição, M. V. Heitor, B.A. Lundvall (eds.), (2003), Innovation, Competence Building, and Social Cohesion in Europe - Towards a Learning Society, London: Edward Elgar. See also, C. Vest (2007), "The American Research University – from World War II to World Wide Web", University of California Press.

[2] P. Conceição, M. V. Heitor, (2005), Innovation for All? Learning from the Portuguese path to technical change and the dynamics of innovation. Westport and London: Praeger.

[3] European Commission (2004). Increasing human resources for science and technology in Europe.Gago, J., Ziman, J., Caro, P., Constantinou, C., Davies, G., Parchmann, I., Rannikmäe, M. and Sjøberg, S. (Eds.); High Level Group on Human Resources for Science and Technology, European Commission.

[4] Miller, S., Caro, P., Koulaidis, V., Semir, V., Staveloz, W. and Vargas, R. (2002). Report from the Expert Group Benchmarking the promotion of RTD culture and Public Understanding of Science. <http://www.jinnove.com/upload/documentaire/PP-fe-106.pdf>

[5] Rodrigues, M.J. (ed., 2002). "The new Knowledge Economy in Europe – A strategy for international competitiveness and social cohesion". Edward Elgar.

[6] P. Conceição, M. V. Heitor, G. Sirilli and R. Wilson (2004), "The Swing of the Pendulum from Public to Market Support for Science and Technology: Is the US Leading the Way?", Technological Forecasting and Social Change, 71(5), pp. 553-578.

[7] Audretsch, D., 2006. *The Entrepreneurial Society*, Oxford University Press.

[8] See Conceição, P. and Heitor, M.V. (2007), "Do we need a revisited policy agenda for research integrity? ...an institutional perspective", "World Conference on Research Integrity", Calouste Gulbenkian Foundation, Lisbon, Portugal, 16-18 September 2007. See also, Conceição, P. and Heitor, M.V. (1999), "On the role of the university in the knowledge-based economy". Science and Public Policy, 26 (1), pp. 37-51.

[9] See also, David, P. and Metcalfe, S. (2007), "Universities and Public Research organizations in the ERA", prepared for the EC (DG-Research) Expert Group on "Knowledge and Growth", June 2007.

[10] Gago, J.M. (2007), Ed., "The Future of Science and Technology in Europe", Portuguese Ministry of Science, Technology and Higher Education.

[11] See, for example, Pavitt, K. (1987), "The Objectives of Technology Policy", *Science and Public Policy*, 14, 182-188; Rosenberg, N. and Nelson, R.

R. (1996), "The Roles of Universities in the Advance of Industrial Technology", in Rosenbloom, R. S. and Spencer, W. J., *Engines of Innovation*. Cambridge, MA: Harvard Business School Press.

[12] Oliveira, P., Conceição, P. and Heitor, M., 1998. "Expectations for the University in the Age of the Knowledge Based Societies" *Technological Forecasting & Social Change*, 58 (3): 203-214

[13] Conceição, P. and Heitor, M. V. (1999). "On the Role of the University in the Knowledge Economy", *Science and Public Policy*, vol. 26, no. 1, pp. 37-51.

[14] UCLA (1997). *The American College Teacher: National Norms for the 1995-96 HERI Faculty Survey*. Los Angeles, CA: Higher Education Research Institute of the University of California at Los Angeles.

[15] Gibbons, M, et al. (1994), *The New Production of Knowledge*, SAGE Publ.

[16] See, for detailed comparative analysis, Abrar Hasan (2007), "Independent legal status and universities as foundations", Paper prepared for the Portuguese Ministry of Science, technology and Higher Education.

[17] Pavitt, K. (1998), "The Social Shaping of the National Science Base," *Research Policy*, 27(8): 793-805.

[18] <http://www.mitportugal.org/>

[19] <http://www.cmuportugal.org/>

[20] <http://www.utaustinportugal.org/>

[21] See, for example, Goodall, A.H. 2006. Should research universities be led by top researchers and are they? Journal of Documentation, 62 (3): 388-411.

[22] Ziman, J. (1968), Public Knowledge: The Social Dimension of Science, Cambridge University Press

[23] Ernst, R. (2003), "The Responsibility of Scientists, a European View", Angew. Chem. Int. Ed. 2003, 42, pp. 4434-4439.

3

The Role of European Regions in the Higher Education Process of the EU

Hans-Jürgen Blinn

"A 'Europe of Knowledge' is impossible without the best minds from all around the world. Universities are the best forums for an intercultural exchange of knowledge that leads to the acquisition of new insights and findings. This is why Germany's universities will continue to make themselves more attractive to highly-qualified students and academics from abroad."

This quote from the President of the German Rectors' Conference, Professor Dr. Margret Wintermantel, is the road-map of the reform-process in the higher education system of Germany and the EU.[1]

Germany's Constitutional System

The name "Federal Republic of Germany" itself denotes the country's federal structure. The Federal Republic consists of 16 Länder (states). The Länder are not mere provinces but states endowed with their own powers. Each has a constitution which must be consistent with the republican, democratic and social principles embodied in the Basic Law, the "Grundgesetz". Subject to these conditions the states can shape their own constitutions.

The federal system has a long tradition in Germany and was interrupted only by the Nazi regime from 1933 until 1945. Germany is one of the classical federal states. Federalism has proved its worth: it is much easier for a country with a federal structure than for a centralized state to take account of regional characteristics and problems. But the main purpose of federalism is to safeguard the nation's freedom. The distribution of responsibilities between the Federation and the states is an essential element of the power-sharing arrangement, the checks and balances, as provided for in the Basic Law. This also embraces the participation of the states in the legislative process at the federal level through the Bundesrat (Federal Council) and playing even a vital role on the European level.

Under an agreement concluded in 1987 between the Federation and the states on the notification and involvement of the Bundesrat and the Länder in European Union affairs, the Bundesrat established in 1988, what is known as, the "EU Chamber" which adopts resolutions on EU documents and bills. The EU-Maastricht Treaty,[2] ratified in December 1992, resulted in an amendment of the German Basic Law (Art. 23)[3] to accord the states greater rights of participation in EU affairs through the Bundesrat and a law, regulating the shared powers in EU affairs between the states and the federal government.[4]

In contrast to the senatorial system of federal states like the United States of America or Switzerland, the Bundesrat does not consist of elected representatives of the people but of members of the state governments or their representatives. Depending on the size of their population, the states have three, four, five or six votes which may only be cast as a block. Rhineland-Palatinate has, for example, 4 votes representing 4 millions inhabitants.

The Basic Law determines the powers of the Federation in terms of whether laws should be the same for all the states or whether the states should be allowed to make their own laws. The states can fill in any gaps left by federal legislation or in areas not specified in the Basic Law. Thus the states are responsible for education and culture almost in their entirety as a manifestation of their "cultural sovereignty".

The real strength of the states lies however in their participation in the legislative process at the federal level through the Bundesrat. All internal administration lies in their hands, and their bureaucracy implements most federal laws and regulations.

However, these legal principles are not without problems. More than half of all bills require the formal approval of the Bundesrat in recent years, which means that they cannot pass into law against will. Therefore many times we had a deadlock between the two parliamentary chambers. The states and the Federal Government have a hard time, for instance, to find ways of financing the higher education system in Germany in respect to the Bologna process.

The 16 German Länder have their regular "Conferences" of a certain type for each of their ministers (e.g. those of culture, higher education, research, interior affaires). Some of them have a standing administrative apparatus at their disposal. Following the founding of the Federal Republic of Germany it soon became clear that there was a basic public need for education to be coordinated and harmonised throughout the country if people were to be provided with the opportunity of mobility between the Länder in their professional and private lives.

The main aim of the cooperation entered into by the Länder in 1948 with the founding of the Standing Conference of the Ministers of Education and Cultural Affairs of the Länder in the Federal Republic of Germany (Kultusministerkonferenz – KMK)[5] was to guarantee, by means of coordination, the necessary measure of shared characteristics and comparability in Germany's education system, an aim that is still pursued to this day, even and especially during the implementation of the Bologna process.

Resolutions of the Standing Conference (KMK) can only be adopted unanimously and regulate mutual acceptance of school diploma, matters of access to university study, quality requirements, planning frameworks and the like. They have the status of recommendations until they are enacted as binding legislation by the parliaments in the Länder. The resolutions are implemented in the individual Länder in the form of administrative acts, ordinances or laws, with the Land parliaments playing a role in the legislative procedure.[6]

The European Higher Education Area

The European Higher Education Area is situated at the crossroads of research, education and innovation which are the key parts of the knowledge triangle. Integral to society at large, it is a central player in the knowledge economy and key to the competitiveness of the EU. In spring 2000 Lisbon's European Council called for Europe's education and training systems to be modernised in response to the demands of the knowledge based economy. The Spring 2002 European Council concluded that the idea of reform is widely embraced, that member states are determined to fully implement the work programme and set themselves the objective of making the European education and training systems a world quality reference by 2010.[7] It took 30 years of cooperation, from the formal adoption of the first Community action programme on education in February 1976, for such recognition to be expressed as clearly as this at the highest level of the Union.[8]

Two of the core indicators used to monitor progress are higher education graduates and cross-national mobility of students in higher education.

At the same time, the intergovernmental Bologna Process focuses specifically on higher education and aims to create a European higher education Area by 2010, in which students can choose from a wide and transparent range of high quality courses and benefit from smooth recognition procedures. The Bologna Declaration of June 1999[9] put in motion a series of reforms needed to make European higher education more compatible and comparable, more competitive and more attractive for Europeans and for students and scholars from other continents. The three key-priorities of the Bologna process are: introduction of the three cycle system (Bachelor/Master/Doctorate); quality assurance; and, recognition of qualifications and periods of study.

There are numerous policy drivers for higher education in the EU. The role of higher education in the Lisbon strategy goes beyond the programme of reforms initiated by the Bologna Declaration. While the Lisbon agenda plays an implicit rather than explicit role in the higher education sector, the role of universities in the knowledge economy is coming under increased scrutiny as they are crucial to the achievement of many Lisbon priorities.

The education ministers of the EU have discussed the need for comprehensive reforms and concluded that in order to successfully reform higher education systems, a comprehensive approach is needed including: curriculum, internal and external governance and funding.

Institutional autonomy should be increased and accompanied by robust governance arrangements with skilled leaders. Employers and students should be actively involved in reform processes, and it is especially important to accept student experience of higher education as central to reform success.[10]

The Bologna Process

On the whole, the Bologna process has a good reputation in Europe and worldwide. It is an extremely important catalyst for change. This explains, why meanwhile 46 countries have joined it: from Iceland to Turkey, from Portugal to Russia, from the UK to Azerbaijan. Montenegro has now signed up to the Bologna Process and became the 46th member in London in 2007 at the 5th bi-annual meeting of all European Ministers of Higher Education. It is nearly the whole Europe united under the umbrella of the Bologna Process. This international cooperation is the only way to open higher education to all students in Europe irrespective of where they are from.

Advisory members are among others the EU Commission, the European Council, the European student organizations, the universities, the social partners and UNESCO. We are lucky not only to include their advice but also to get impulses from them. Unlike these advisory members the Bologna process is not an organization, although it is well organized. But it resembles a flying carpet with virtual power rather than a body issuing directives, laws or using other legal instruments. There is no authority at the European level, which represents the Bologna process apart from the conference of ministers. They decide upon a Communiqué, that has no legally binding effect.

The Bologna Process has a strong impact on the development of higher education in Europe.[11] It has helped to modernize universities as well as our higher education systems and will hopefully do so in the future. We are steadily achieving comparability between the degree systems, improving the recognition of awarded qualifications as well as the quality of provisions to students and staff gathering experiences in other countries. The newest "Stocktaking Report on the Bologna Process"[12] prepared for the London Ministerial meeting states in two conclusions:

– There has been good progress in the Bologna Process since Bergen 2005. This means we can see considerable progress in achieving the core goals such as the comparability of the degree systems, the improvement of quality assurance and of recognition.
– The outlook for achieving the goals by 2010 is good, but there are still some challenges to be faced.

Over the last four years, European universities have adapted their degree programmes to meet new European structures, as outlined under the Bologna Declaration, in rapidly increasing numbers. According to a survey of 900 institutions, 82 % of European universities now offer Bologna-compliant degree structures – up from 53 % four years ago. The latest Bologna progress report was conducted by the European Universities Association[13] and released in early May. The report concludes that a tipping point has been reached "where it is no longer relevant to question whether or not structural reforms will take place."

Other findings of the survey show that only 2 % of European universities do not plan to adopt the new three-year Bachelor's and two-year Master's degrees – down from 7.5 % four years ago; while intra-European credit transfer has become somewhat easier. However, mobility patterns are unequal. In five countries – Britain, Finland, Ireland, Malta and Sweden – at least 80 % of colleges report a significant increase in the number of students from other countries coming in than native students going abroad. Countries with the opposite experience are Bosnia-Herzegovina, Bulgaria, Lithuania, Poland and Turkey.

The progress made in the different member states is of course different following from the fact that the beginning of the memberships dates back to different years. Also the speed of progress is different. But more or less every country tries its best.

As far as Germany is concerned we can realize a lot of progress but nevertheless also some opposition in the universities against several goals of the Bologna Process. Since the amendment to the Framework Act of Higher Education (Hochschulrahmengesetz) of 1998[14], higher education institutions are also entitled to award Bachelor's and Master's degrees independently of any cooperation with foreign institutions of higher education. The new Bachelor's and Master's programmes meanwhile account for a 48% share of all degree programmes. The universities meanwhile offer 41% of their extensive overall catalogue of studies in the multi-cycle academic format of Bologna; and at universities of applied sciences, the proportion of Bachelor's and Master's programmes actually amounts to 74%. The transition of the remaining degree programmes is in progress, with the exception of some state-regulated degree courses.

Still, some professors predict a process of downgrading quality of the higher education system. Some professors fear
- the change to a study structure that has unforeseeable results,
- the change to a qualification/ learning outcomes oriented system,
- the bureaucracy of the quality assurance methods and
- the competition with other countries and systems.

Some of them fail to notice the possibility of getting more flexibility in the study programmes of the two cycle structure as well as in the combination of learning phases than in the diploma study programmes. And in some parts they do not accept the necessity of more cooperation between higher education and industry, the necessity of improving the quality of teaching and learning.

After Bologna in 1999, where the 29 European Ministers for Higher Education agreed upon the Bologna Declaration and after Prague in 2001, Berlin in 2003, Bergen in 2005 they met in 2007 in London for the fifth time.[15] The next meeting in 2009 will take place in Leuven in Belgium hosted by the Benelux States. In its heading the London Communiqué refers to two developments and goals:
- to reaching the European Higher Education Area and
- to responding to the challenges of the globalized world.

It also takes into account the depth of the process both to the extent of reforms at the European, at the national and institutional level. It includes the different goals as there are improving, the two cycle degree structure, including the Doctoral studies as the third cycle, and employability improving quality and quality assurance and the recognition of qualifications implementing a qualifications framework and the social dimension of students.

The European countries are committed to creating a European Higher Education Area (EHEA) by 2010 aiming at facilitating more mobility of students and scientific staff and improving the competitive power of the European higher education sector in the global competition. At the same time it is not intended to harmonize the different cultures, structures and systems of the European countries. Every member state wants to keep and should preserve its cultural identity and heritage.

On the other hand creating a European Higher Education Area requires having certain standards in common, such as the two cycle degree system. Important prerequisite for mobility and for offering - for example - joint cross border study programmes are mutual reliability and transparency. Quality assurance plays an important role in this context, one could even say: quality assurance is a corner stone of the Bologna process.

Globalization and Employability

The globalization of the economies has not become one of the main contents of the London Communiqué. Nevertheless it is a virtual reference point for the process.

In 2000 the European Union accepted the Lisbon Agenda to make Europe the most competitive and dynamic knowledge economy in the world by 2010. This strategy shall increase employment across the EU. Many businesses are trading in the global marketplace, not only multinational groups but also the small and medium sized companies.

The internet opens these markets to every pharmacy or bookshop; the trading paths require law firms giving advice around the world. The Siemens Corporation has production units and branches in 195 states of the world, think of car producers (you learn from failures as well: DaimlerChrysler), of Microsoft, airlines, oil companies.

For companies to acquire the skills and competencies they need and for their employees to step up in their careers the European countries need to improve education and in particular higher education in all professions.

This is not possible without the reference to international orientation. Even looking at the third cycle, the doctorate, companies ask for international experience and project management, for example in the technical disciplines. If higher education is to boost competitiveness and growth in the European economies the necessity of cooperating with the industry and the employer's side is obvious. When designing study programmes and qualifications the dialogue with chambers and professional associations is essential.

In this context the London Communiqué addresses the question of employability. That means each degree students are awarded should enable them to find an adequate occupation. This is not only in the interest of the industry but of utmost importance for the graduate. "We urge institutions to further develop partnerships and cooperation with employers in the ongoing process of curriculum innovation based on learning outcomes."[16]

But when looking at the introduction of the London Communiqué you will find the international orientation not being reduced on economic references. "Building on our rich and diverse European cultural heritage, we are developing a European Higher Education Area based on institutional autonomy, academic freedom, equal opportunities and democratic principles that will facilitate mobility, increase employability and strengthen Europe's attractiveness and competitiveness." This wording makes clear: The Bologna Process is not one-dimensional.

Education and the General Agreement on Trade in Services (GATS)

Education is still largely a national affair, even though the level of private sector penetration may vary from country to country, but it is fast becoming a worldwide service industry too, even for publicly-funded systems. Traded educational services are already a major business in some countries (for example, in Australia, New Zealand and the United States, they are respectively the third, fourth and fifth largest service export).[17]

This area has grown because of the increasing number of students travelling to study abroad. There are reputedly over two million students studying outside their country of origin, usually paying substantial annual fees to foreign institutions. The economy of this trade is being affected by the growth of information and communication technology (ICT) which is being used by educational institutions (public universities) and private education companies to develop competitive advantage in international markets and delivery over rivals. Higher education institutions, operating in consortia, sometimes with major media corporations, appear to be competing within global markets for new income opportunities (for example, the University of California Los Angeles [UCLA] Extension school in the U.S. offers around 50 courses over the Web to students in 44 U.S. states and in 8 countries).

Both the OECD and the EU have tended to view this marketization process as "natural" and as a trade question. In this way, apart from recording the growth of this sector, they focused upon the difficulties of the non-recognition of the varied diplomas/degrees granted by foreign providers (which will affect market development and the expected gains). A new global educational market may emerge that will challenge current national quality assurance and accreditation systems.

A the same time, convergent European policies, opening out the Community as a dynamic economic area, and recognizing the growth of the service sector and the shift to the new knowledge economy, have used or licensed private sector partnerships to manage or even own parts of the education service. The General Agreement on Trade in Services (GATS[18]) started some years ago as an attempt to manage the trade in education services between countries[19]. Because of the complex nature of education in public/ private partnerships today, this has implications for the local as well as international market in education.[20]

The question is, whether education as a public good, can be treated as tradable like steel or pharmaceuticals? And whether, in the globalizing corporate economy, regulated national education sectors will be subordinated to intensive profit regimes? The United States, Australia and New Zealand have all submitted proposals for the next round of WTO[21] talks on services, which are in a deadlock because of the negotiations in the agricultural field.

In broad terms, the proposals are designed to make it easier for private universities to expand across borders and for students to move more freely overseas to choose their university. Australia, for example, cites laws in some countries limiting foreign ownership of private educational institutions and onerous visa requirements as barriers to trade in educational services. The proposals are very controversial and are being stiffly resisted by student organizations and other nongovernmental groups which say it is not up to trade negotiators in Geneva to discuss how countries educate their people.

There are various social objectives that make higher education different from, say, hairdressing. In my opinion, education is a public good and it needs to be treated as a public good. Partly because of lobbying from NGO's, the European Commission, which negotiates on behalf of the European Union, ruled out any deal on education in the present GATS trade round. But for how long it will stand, nobody knows. One reason Europe is not proposing to further open its educational sector is because it has already liberalized it considerably. During the last round of service-sector trade talks, in 1994, the EU made commitments to open its markets for private primary, secondary and tertiary education – a move not yet taken by the United States or Japan.

The fact that Europe will not make any concessions during this round does not preclude other countries from doing so. Under the WTO system, countries negotiate packages: The United States, for example, might agree to remove barriers to its educational market if Europe agrees to liberalize its transport sector. The WTO talks are meant to deal only with private education; there is a consensus that state-owned universities should not be touched. But experts say the line between private and public is becoming increasingly blurred. Partnerships between private companies and public universities are common, especially in the research field, and public schools sometimes seek private companies for certain services like computer classes.

"It's something which is not very clear," said Kurt Larsen, a specialist in the field who works at the OECD (Organization for Economic Cooperation and Development) in Paris. "Trade people don't want that to be very clear," he said. This is partly because it might mean limiting the scope for liberalization. China, a newcomer to the WTO, is pursuing "a very open policy on educational services," Larsen said[22]. Chinese authorities allow foreign universities to operate in the country as long as they partner with a local university. The largest "exporters" of educational services are the United States, Britain and Australia. These countries are active in both attracting students to their own campuses and opening campuses abroad. Receiving foreign students is a highly lucrative business because the receiving country benefits from the students paying not only tuition, but living expenses and travel – the equivalent in some ways of big-spending tourists.

Altogether the OECD puts the global market for such "educational services" at about $30 billion, which is only slightly less than the worldwide market for financial services. It is these huge financial stakes that have convinced countries like the United States, Australia and New Zealand to put proposals on the table. For New Zealand, a relatively small economy, "educational services" are the fourth largest revenue earner for its service sector. One of the New Zealand government's proposals is to make it easier for student recruitment and placement services to operate across borders. "The reduction of barriers to trade in education does not equate to an erosion of core public education systems and standards", the government says in its proposal.

But groups opposed to mixing trade talks with education say the highly intangible notion of educational "quality" may suffer if education is treated on a purely commercial basis. Trade negotiators have dollars in mind, not quality, they say. Emma Hughes of People and Planet[23] offers a litany of potential pitfalls: "We don't want low-demand academic courses to get neglected", she said. "We're concerned about academic freedom – that it doesn't become dependent on who is holding the purse strings. We're concerned about making sure that students from poor backgrounds can get access to education." "Basically," she said, "citizens of all countries should have the right to regulate vital services." A number of countries have studied the idea of putting "quality assurance" clauses into trade agreements.

The Norwegian government is particularly concerned about this because it sends large numbers of students overseas every year – and is able to pay their tuition thanks largely to oil revenues. But the government would like to know that it is getting a minimum level of "quality" at universities overseas. Together with Australia, the Norwegian government convened representatives late last year from more than a dozen countries to discuss the idea of quality assurance. The topic is so sensitive that the talks were held in secret, but as you see, not secretly enough. Those familiar with the discussions say that participants effectively concluded that the world is not yet ready to rate educational quality the way you might label bed sheets by their thread count or a computer by its processing speed.

The London Communiqué

A main reference point of the London Communiqué is getting the European Higher Education Area up and functioning by 2010. This is one of the main goals of the Bologna Process. We have done quite a lot during the last eight years.

The Stocktaking Report 2007 makes clear: Good progress has been made. But at the same time there is still some way to go. This includes two fields of activities.

The first is: We need to continue our endeavours to make the Process reality at the national and the institutional level, which means in the universities. The two cycle system, quality assurance, ECTS, modulization, qualification frameworks and other requirements have to be implemented as far and quickly as possible. We are aiming at fulfilling a substantial quantity of goals by 2010. Ministers in London asked for concentrating the reforms on improving the experience of students. By the end of their studies they should be in the best position to get a job. This focus on learning outcomes should facilitate learning on an international scale.

The second point is how to design and to define the European Higher Education Area cornerstones for the time beyond 2010. In the ministerial meeting the comments on this challenge have been reluctant because it is not useful to develop definitions and goals without thorough preparation. During the London Conference Ministers and other stakeholders had the opportunity to discuss the future of the European Higher Education Area in parallel panels. It was quite interesting to see that these discussions concentrated after a short while on present problems and challenges. This happened because the future is in some parts still far away and furthermore it is of course very difficult to think for and in the far future, 10 or 15 years ahead.

We need and want a European Higher Education Area which sees the recent developments as an ongoing process. We learn from the industry: a company which cannot change with the times is unlikely to survive and I think this is true for the higher education sector as well.

Social Dimension

One of the most important subjects of the preparing discussions as well as in the Ministerial meeting was the social dimension.

The social dimension refers to three orientations:

–   first to the participation of students in the process of higher education at all levels,
–   a second element is the funding, the financial and social help for students within a country and for studying abroad,
–   a third point refers to the available data.

To the first point: Participation of students at all levels describes a requirement that has to reflect the diversity of cultures and populations. Nevertheless apart from theses differences it would not be in line with these principles to say: there is no participation possible. It is necessary to secure student's participation within the culture of managing a university; students should be part of the quality assurance process, for example.

The funding is always a very delicate matter. Without sufficient funding no mobility is possible. The preconditions as well as the cultures and systems of funding are very different, in one country it includes tax reductions for the parents, in another one students receive a direct payment. Apart from that funding subsidies and scholarships is essential for student's access to higher education without obstacles related to their social and economic background.

Missing is a survey about the whole European Higher Education Area. What we therefore have to do first is to gather data on that. Ministers have asked to report on the social strategies and policies for the social dimension and to develop comparable indicators and data to measure progress towards the overall objective for the social dimension and student and staff mobility in all Bologna countries. The Bologna member states will also continue their efforts to provide adequate student services. In Germany it is the "Deutsches Studentenwerk", which covers the social student services and they do a very good job.

Quality Assurance

One of the crucial points of an international system of cooperation is mutual reliability. Therefore we need to provide reliable quality assurance systems at the national level and some cross border information about it. In Bergen Ministers had agreed on the principle of a European Register on quality assurance agencies. The purpose of the register is to allow all stakeholders an open access to information about trustworthy agencies. The register will be voluntary, self-financing, independent and transparent. Agencies will have to pay fees for being admitted to the register. Meanwhile the European Quality Assurance Register for Higher Education (EQAR) has been founded on 4 March 2008 as an independent organization in charge of establishing and managing a register of quality assurance agencies.[24]

Erasmus Mundus II - The Reference for International Cooperation in Higher Education

The European Commission adopted in 2007 a proposal to launch the new generation of the Erasmus Mundus programme for the period 2009-2013.[25]

Erasmus Mundus started in 2004 to promote European higher education as a centre of excellence in the world. In the first three academic years, 2,325 third-country students (third-country = non-EU-countries) from over 100 countries and 323 universities in and outside Europe have successfully participated in the programme and an additional 1,826 students will start their studies in Europe in September.

The new Erasmus Mundus II programme builds on this by aiming to become the EU reference programme for cooperation with third countries in this area. Over a period of five years, just over 950 million euros will be available for European and third-country universities to join forces in joint programmes or collaborative partnerships, and to grant scholarships to European and third-country students for an international study experience.

The current Erasmus Mundus programme has been successfully running since its launch in 2004, encouraging the creation of high-quality Masters courses in Europe and attracting high calibre students from third countries to European universities. Erasmus Mundus has been an important contributor to the modernisation of EU's universities in a context of globalization of higher education issues, which relates to the Bologna Process.

This new approach translates into a whole range of new programme activities which cover joint Doctoral programmes, increased financial support for European students, as well as collaborative partnerships with specific world regions to the benefit of all partners involved.

The Commission has thus decided to consolidate the current activities while also extending them and adding a new dimension to the programme. The activities of the new programme will be:

– the support of joint programmes of outstanding academic quality at Master's and Doctoral level, including a scholarship scheme for high-calibre EU and third-country students and academics;
– the promotion of partnerships between European and third-country universities in specific world regions as a basis for structured cooperation, transfer of know-how, exchange and mobility at all levels of higher education;
– the support of measures which will help to enhance the worldwide appeal of Europe as an educational destination.

The main novelties of the programme proposal are:

– more opportunities and variety in the institutional cooperation modalities between European and third-country universities and in the individual mobility scheme;
– extension of Erasmus Mundus to doctoral studies and, partially, to the undergraduate level;
– stronger financial support for European students through the offer of more attractive scholarships.

The new programme has been adopted by the Commission and voted for by the European Parliament in October 2008 and will enter into force in the academic year 2009/2010 when the current programme expires.

Perspectives

There are a lot of other recommendations in the Communiqué of the London Conference and as a result, London has brought substantial progress to the Bologna Process. In the course of the national reform discussions in Germany, we have occasionally lost sight of the task of facilitating international mobility. We must work more determinedly on modernising degree programmes as well as forms of learning, and on structuring these more clearly. But we must also be more courageous and flexible in our efforts, and must certainly also adapt our organisational structures and processes.

The institutions of higher education are facing great challenges in Germany: on the one hand, higher education must be modernized within the framework of the Bologna reform, on the other hand, the number of persons qualified to enter higher education will rise considerably until 2020. In order to maintain the performance of institutions of higher education and to keep them open for a larger number of new entrants, the Federal Government and the Länder agreed to basic elements of a Higher Education Pact. The goal of this Pact is to create alone 91,000 additional study places in the old federal states of western Germany by 2010 and will receive therefore a share of 565 Mio. € of federal funds.

By promoting top-class university research within the framework of the Initiative for Excellence, the Federal Government is aiming to establish internationally visible research beacons in Germany. 1.9 billion € will be made available to the institutions of higher education within the framework of the Initiative for Excellence.[26] The evaluations will be implemented by the German Research Association and the Science Council. The final decisions for the first round of funding were published in 2006 and two universities in Munich and one in Karlsruhe were the winners. In fall 2007 a second round of drafts have been followed.[27]

To reach the European Higher Education Area is a long and winding road to travel, but the German Länder will play their vital role in this process to make it a success in the end.

Endnotes

[1] Press release (38/06), German Rectors' Conference, Bonn, 29 June 2006; <http://www.hrk.de/eng>

[2] Official Journal No. C 191 from 29 July 1992

[3] Gesetz zur Änderung des Grundgesetzes vom 21. Dezember 1992 (BGBl. I S. 2086) und Gesetz zur Änderung des Grundgesetzes vom 28. August 2006 (BGBl. I S. 2034)

[4] Gesetz über die Zusammenarbeit von Bund und Ländern in Angelegenheiten der Europäischen Union vom 12. März 1993 (BGBl. I S. 313, 1780), zuletzt geändert durch das Föderalismusreform-Begleitgesetz vom 5. September 2006 (BGBl. I S. 2098) und Vereinbarung zwischen der Bundesregierung und den Regierungen der Länder über die Zusammenarbeit in Angelegenheiten der Europäischen Union in Ausführung von § 9 des Gesetzes über die Zusammenarbeit von Bund und Ländern in Angelegenheiten der Europäischen Union vom 29. Oktober 1993 (Bundesanzeiger Nr. 226 v. 2. Dezember 1993, S. 10425 f; Bundesanzeiger Nr. 123 v. 8. Juli 1998, S. 9433)

[5] Geschäftsordnung der Ständigen Konferenz der Kultusminister der Länder in der Bundesrepublik Deutschland gemäß Beschluss vom 19. November 1955 i.d.F. vom 2. Juni 2005; <http://www.kmk.org>

[6] The Education System in the Federal Republic of Germany 2005, Standing Conference of the Ministers of Education and Cultural Affairs, Bonn, 2005

[7] Conclusions of the Barcelona European Council, 15-16 March 2002, § 43

[8] The History of European Cooperation in Education and Training, Europe in the making – an example, Official Publication of the European Communities, Luxembourg, 2006, p. 21

[9] The European Higher Education Area, Joint Declaration of the European Ministers of Education, The Bologna Declaration of 19 June 1999, Bologna

[10] Progress towards the Lisbon Objectives in Education and Training, Staff working document of the European Commission, Brussels, May 16, 2006, Brussels SEC (2006) 639

[11] Focus on the Structure of Higher Education in Europe 2006/07, National Trends in the Bologna Process, EURYDICE, Brussels, 2007

[12] Bologna Process Stocktaking Report 2007, report from a working group appointed by the Bologna-Follow-Up-Group to the Ministerial Conference in London, 17-18 May 2007

[13] <http://www.eua.be>

[14] Hochschulrahmengesetz vom 26. Januar 1976 (BGBl. I S. 185), in der Fassung der Bekanntmachung vom 9. April 1987 (BGBl. I S. 1170), zuletzt

geändert durch Artikel 1 des Gesetzes vom 20. August 1998 (BGBl. I S. 2190)

[15] Bologna 5th Ministerial Conference in London, 17.-18. May 2007; <http://www.dfes.gov.uk/londonbologna/>

[16] The London Communiqué, § 3.5

[17] OECD, Online Education Database, <http://www.oecd.org>

[18] Allgemeine Übereinkommen über den Handel mit Dienstleistungen (GATS) vom 15. April 1994 (BGBl. II, S. 1643 ff.)

[19] Hans-Jürgen Blinn, "Bildung als globale Dienstleistung – Nach der WTO-Konferenz in Hongkong", Zeitschrift für Erwachsenenbildung (DIE), Bonn, Nr. 2, 2006, S. 26-28

[20] Hans-Jürgen Blinn, "Staatliche Kulturförderung und freier Markt, Rechtspolitische Entwicklungen im Rahmen des EU-Gemeinschaftsrechts und des WTO/GATS-Abkommens", Jahrbuch für Kulturpolitik 2007, Band 7 – Europäische Kulturpolitik, Institut für Kulturpolitik der Kulturpolitischen Gesellschaft e.V., Bernd Wagner und Norbert Sievers (Hrsg.), Klartext Verlag, Essen, 2007, S. 175-186

[21] <http://www.wto.org>

[22] Larsen, Kurt, Martin, John P. and Morris, Rosemary, "Trade in Educational Services: Trends and Emerging Issues", The World Economy, Vol. 25, pp. 849-868, 2002

[23] People & Planet is the largest, student network in Britain campaigning to end world poverty, defend human rights and protect the environment. <http://www.peopleandplanet.org>

[24] <http://www.eqar.eu>

[25] Proposal for a Decision of the European Parliament and of the Council establishing an Action Programme for the Enhancement of Quality in Higher Education and the Promotion of Intercultural Understanding through Co-operation with Third Countries (Erasmus Mundus) (2009-2013), Brussels, 12 July 2007, COM(2007)395 final, <http://ec.europa.eu/education/programmes/mundus>

[26] <http://www.bmbf.de/de/1321.php>

[27] Meanwhile the following universities were chosen: Heidelberg, Freiburg, Konstanz, FU Berlin, Göttingen, RWTH Aachen

The University Quality Challenge

4

Quality Education and Training in Public Administration
– The Contribution of the University of Speyer –

Siegfried Magiera

The German System of Public Administration and Education as the Frame of Reference for the University of Speyer

The German University of Administrative Sciences Speyer (Deutsche Hochschule für Verwaltungswissenschaften Speyer) is unique for two reasons. The first is its rather long name which only insiders will easily remember. Therefore, I shall use here the shortened term "University of Speyer". The second reason is its place and function in the German system of public administration and education. In order to fully understand the specific role of the University of Speyer, some basic knowledge of the German system is necessary. Therefore, I shall begin my presentation with some remarks on this general background. In the second part, I shall come to the status, organization and function of the University of Speyer, and in the third part to its main activities.

The German System of Public Administration

The German system of public administration can be viewed from different angles. For our purpose three aspects are relevant – the federal system of government, the different categories of public officials, and the different levels of public service positions.

Germany is a federal state. It consists of the Federation (Bund) and – since reunification in 1990 – of sixteen States (Länder). Both, Federation and States, follow the traditional pattern of separation of powers in a parliamentary system of government. Both have their own branches of legislative, executive and judicial institutions with the necessary officeholders. Within the States a second level of administration exists in the form of local governments which have their own public personnel. In addition, at all levels of government, various corporate bodies and institutions of public law have been established for specific tasks and with a staff of their own.

The public service at all levels of government is divided into two categories of officials dependent on whether their status is governed by public law or by private law. The first category applies to the professional civil servants and also to judges and to regular soldiers. The second category comprises ("white-collar") office employees and ("blue-collar") workers. The distinction between the two categories has its origin in the federal constitution, according to which the exercise of public authority as a permanent function shall be generally entrusted to members of the public service whose status is governed by public law. In practice, however, the difference between the two categories, especially between professional civil servants and office employees, has narrowed considerably. Many functions in the public service are exercised equally by members of both groups, although their status is still governed either by public or by private law.

The public service is furthermore divided into different levels of positions. The professional civil service comprises four career groups in vertical order – the basic, the clerical, the managerial and the executive service. A similar – although more flexible – differentiation exists for the positions of office employees.

The German System of Education

For the purpose of public administration education, the German system of education can be divided into general education, and specific education for the public service.

General education falls into the competence of the States. Primary and secondary education is provided by public schools, higher education by public colleges and universities. Private schools as well as private colleges and universities are a rare exception. Entrance into the different career groups of the professional civil service depends on certain minimum requirements of formal education. These are diplomas or their equivalent from a primary school for the basic service, from a middle-school for the clerical service, from a secondary school for the managerial service, and from a university for the executive service.

General education is a necessary requirement to enter the public service, but not a sufficient foundation to exercise the specific functions within the public service. Therefore, the federal, state and local governments have established various forms and institutions for additional training of their personnel. Examples are the Federal Academy for Public Administration (Bundesakademie für öffentliche Verwaltung) or the professional colleges for public administration (Fachhochschulen für öffentliche Verwaltung) of the Federation and the States. They differ from the general colleges and universities not only in their functions, but also in their status. In contrast to the latter, they are an integral part of the federal or state governments and do not enjoy academic autonomy and the right of self-government.

Status, Organization and Function of the University of Speyer

After this broad outline of the German system of public administration and education, the question arises as to the place of the University of Speyer in this intricate system. In summary, one can say that the University of Speyer is an academic institution equal in status and organization to the universities in general, but with functions specifically designed to meet the needs of the public service.

Status

The University of Speyer was founded in 1947 by the French authorities in occupied Germany as "Ecole Supérieure d'Administration" (Höhere Verwaltungsakademie) according to the model of the Ecole Nationale d'Administration in Paris. Incidentally, the latter moved to Strasbourg, only 75 miles away from Speyer, at the beginning of 1992. After the reorganization of the western part of Germany by the Basic Law of 1949, the "Speyer Academy" was transformed into an institution owned and operated jointly by the Federation and the States of the newly established Federal Republic. The status of the re-named "Postgraduate School of Administrative Sciences Speyer" was formalized in a specific act passed by the legislature of the State of Rhineland-Palatinate.

Like the universities in general, the University of Speyer is a public corporation and a state institution. It has the right of self-government within the limits of the law including the right to enact its own by-laws. Accordingly, the University of Speyer has adopted general regulations for its basic order and special rules, inter alia, for its elections, its admission and examination procedures, and its library.

Like the universities in general, the University of Speyer is subject to a limited legal supervision of its self-government by the Ministry of Education, Science, Youth and Culture of the State of Rhineland-Palatinate. In its academic work it is protected by constitutional law, especially by Art. 5 para. 3 of the German Basic Law, according to which art and science, research and teaching are free, although freedom of teaching does not absolve one from loyalty to the constitution.

Organization

The organization of the University of Speyer follows the general pattern for universities. Members are the professors, the assistants, the students, and the administrative staff. As to the professors, the University of Speyer has positions only in the highest category according to German law. At present, there are 18 chairs in the areas of public law, economics, public administration, and other social sciences, such as political science, sociology and modern history. All chairs are endowed with a full-time assistant and a full-time secretary. In addition, the professors are members of the German Research Institute for Public Administration (Deutsches Forschungsinstitut für öffentliche Verwaltung) attached to the University.

Administrative organs of the University are the Senate, the President (Rektor), and the Board of Trustees (Verwaltungsrat). The Senate is composed of the President, the Vice-President, and delegates of the different member groups. It takes care of all fundamental affairs of the University unless they are explicitly entrusted to other organs. The President is elected for four years from the group of professors by the Senate. He is the head of the University and responsible to the Senate. The Board of Trustees consists of representatives of the Federation, the States, and the President and Vice-President of the University. It supports the University in fulfilling its tasks; however, in certain matters enumerated by law mutual agreement must be established between the University and the Board of Trustees.

Function

As to their functions, there is a noticeable difference between the University of Speyer and other universities. In general, universities serve the development of science by research, teaching and studying. They also prepare for professional careers which require the application of scientific findings and methods. The University of Speyer is entrusted with an additional and more specific function. It forms a centre of administrative sciences for research and offers postgraduate studies for advanced and continuing education in these fields.

Activities of the University of Speyer

For the last part of my presentation, I shall now turn to the activities of the University of Speyer. Due to its unique position in the German system and to the various academic disciplines represented by its faculty, these activities cover a wide range of research projects, course subjects, and teaching methods. For a better understanding and in order to keep within the given time limit, I shall restrict myself to a summary of the major activities.

Teaching Activities

Teaching activities are performed by the professors and by out-standing practitioners. They cover pre-service education and in-service education. The courses and conferences cater to persons interested or involved in the public service of all branches of government. The general requirement for participation is a university degree; for specific courses and conferences additional requirements may apply, such as a senior or a specialized position in the public service.

The teaching staff comprises – in addition to the 18 permanent professors – some 80 guest lecturers and a large number of ad hoc speakers. This mixture guarantees a fruitful exchange of academic and practical experience as well as course work in small groups. The lecturers and speakers are generally high ranking practitioners from German, foreign, and international institutions. Among them are the presidents of the European Court of Justice, the German Federal Constitutional Court, the German Federal Bank, and the German Federal Court of Auditors. Some are also honorary professors or hold an honorary doctorate of our University. Regular semesters and major conferences are usually opened with an address by government members or other top officials. Among these have been the presidents of the European Parliament and of the European Commission, the Federal Chancellor, state prime ministers, and chairmen of well-known business corporations. A former Federal President is a retired member of the faculty, while another held an honorary doctorate of the University.

Pre-service education comprises three types of programs for post-graduate participants – the Speyer Semester, the Master's program, and doctoral studies.

The *Speyer Semester* is a three-month program offered in the summer and in the winter. It is certified by federal and state law as an integral part of the two-year practical training of law school graduates who are state employees while they prepare for their second state examination, but other university graduates may also participate. The program includes all areas of administrative sciences covered by the faculty and complementary language and oratory courses. In-depth courses are offered for participants who want to specialize in particular fields, such as public management or European and international affairs. Successful completion of the program requires minimum attendance of twenty hours of class work per week and at least passing grades in one seminar offered by a professor and one project study group offered mainly by practitioners.

The program for the degree of *Master of Administrative Sciences* takes one full year and is open to university graduates who have finished their studies with an above-average record. In order to qualify for the degree, participants must successfully complete the program of two Speyer semesters, take part in practical training at an administrative agency, and pass an examination. The latter consists of a thesis written over a period of six weeks and an oral examination. The study plan of each candidate must include classes covering the fundamentals of public administration and two other areas. These can be selected from a total of five particular study fields, such as government and economy or science management. By adding a third semester of study at a European partner university, candidates can earn the supplementary degree of "European Master of Public Administration". In 1982 the Master's program was extended to applicants of foreign, especially developing, countries who seek to improve their qualification for public service in their home countries.

Studies for the degree of *Doctor of Administrative Sciences, of Law, or of Economics and Social Sciences* require successful completion of two Speyer semesters. Candidates must have finished their university studies with a clearly above-average record, write a dissertation, and pass an oral examination covering the subject areas of their dissertation and one other field of administrative sciences. Since 1972 more than 300 doctoral degrees have been awarded by the University.

To complete this report on academic degrees, I should like to mention that the University of Speyer has also been able to qualify 20 postdoctoral candidates by the so-called *habilitation* procedure for a career as a university professor. Most of these candidates have been appointed to academic positions at other universities. Also, assistants – after finishing their temporary employment at one of the academic chairs, especially those who obtain a master's degree or a doctorate at the University – have generally been very successful in finding attractive positions in the public service or the business sector.

In-service education is offered in a variety of forms on a regular or ad hoc basis. The programs are developed in close cooperation with competent institutions of the public service.

In order to guarantee the high standard of quality expected, all *courses and conferences* are initiated and organized by the professors and coordinated by the Senate Committee on Continuing Education. Experts from academic and government institutions are invited as speakers. The number of participants ranges from 25 or fewer at seminars and work shops to more than a hundred at conferences.

An especially ambitious form of continuing education has been institutionalized in a separate *Management College*. It was established in 1991 by the State of Rhineland-Palatinate and has been joined thus far by eight other States and the Federal Employment Agency. The program is meant for public officials who are designated for top executive positions in their States. It consists of 12 one-week courses over a period of two years and includes a practical training period in a business enterprise, a foreign country, or an international organization. One of the special features of the program is that the participants keep their regular positions while participating at the Management College.

Research Activities

Research Activities are pursued, as at universities in general, by the professors and their assistants within the framework of the individual academic chairs.

Furthermore, research activities are pursued within the framework of the *German Research Institute for Public Administration.* The Institute was established in 1976 as a separate entity attached to the University. It is financed equally by the Federation and by the States. Its more than 40 ordinary and corresponding members are professors of the University of Speyer and of other German and foreign universities. Research assistants are hired for specific projects on a temporary basis. At present, the Institute has 18 regular positions for research assistants. The administrative organs of the Institute are the Managing Board composed of at least five professors and two research assistants, the Director, the Scientific Advisory Council, composed of at least three external professors, and the Board of Trustees consisting of representatives of the Federation and the States.

Research projects are initiated by the professors or taken up by them at the request of outside institutions, especially government agencies. All projects must be approved by the Managing Board and carried out or supervised by one or more professors. The research activities are coordinated by the Managing Board in cooperation with the Board of Trustees and laid down in a five-year program. This is annually revised and complemented by a work plan for the current year. For reasons of transparency, individual projects are arranged in three sections: modernizing government and administration; administration in multi-level government; administration between public and private actors.

In distinction to research done at the individual academic chairs, projects at the Institute focus on an interdisciplinary approach and are often carried out by two or more professors of different academic disciplines. The same approach is followed at the conferences and workshops held under the auspices of the Institute, as well as at the regular research colloquia. There, new projects are presented by the research assistants at an early stage in order to receive input from the other members of the Institute.

After their completion, the research projects are published either in regular commercial publications which comprise more than 200 volumes, or in the Institute's own series called Speyer Research Reports (Speyerer Forschungsberichte) which includes more than 250 issues. Furthermore, the University of Speyer has published nearly 200 booklets in its series Speyer Working Papers (Speyerer Arbeitshefte), and almost 200 volumes in its commercial publication series (Schriftenreihe der Hochschule Speyer).

Conclusion

This lengthy and still incomplete report on the University of Speyer was meant to give a general impression of its status and activities within the German system of public administration and education. One of the main principles of the University and its academic staff is to adapt their work to new challenges in the public sector. This can be achieved successfully only in coordination and cooperation with similar institutions at home and abroad.

5

Study and Work Experience: Delinking and Relinking

Frans-Bauke van der Meer
Arthur Ringeling

Introduction

In the practice of public administration there is an increasing need for insight in the nature and causes of societal problems. Also the need for knowledge of the conditions for and impact of public policies is growing, as is the quest for methods for effective governance in multi-actor contexts. The diversity and turbulence of value patterns and societal developments make the nature of societal problems and the dynamics of policy processes increasingly hard to grasp. New administrative arrangements or strategies, new modes of interactive and cooperative policy-making and new substantive policies, therefore, frequently have unanticipated and scarcely understood consequences. It is understandable, then, that many practitioners in the public domain are looking for reflection on and new approaches to their day-to-day practice. The part time program in Public Administration we run in Rotterdam is one response to this need, for which there appears to be a continuous en substantially growing demand.

However, at the same time academic Public Administration research and theory is much criticized for its lack of practical relevance or utilization. Practitioners often find scholarly analysis and prescriptions too theoretical and too general. While at the same time scholars are astonished and sometimes disappointed that politicians and administrators do not incorporate "evident" scientific findings in their strategies. The extensive literature on "utilization" of social science research stems from this astonishment.[1]

Although it is plausible that scientific knowledge often somehow finds its way towards policy processes in the long run, and it is obvious that scientific reports are sometimes used to legitimate (or fight) existing policies, it is clear that there are serious problems in the communication between "science" and "practice". These problems, too, manifest themselves in post-experience MPA programs. As a consequence, key questions[2] become:

–   how can we make our teaching more recognizable and relevant for practitioners?
–   how can we help practitioners to link their practice to their study experiences and vice versa?
–   how can the practical relevance of Public Administration research and theory be enhanced and made tangible for practitioners?

Although the last question may be the most important, in this paper we will focus on the first two, since these are directly related to the design and management of MPA programs. The third question is potentially a nice subject for a separate study in the future.

Outline

In the next section of this paper we will describe our view on what it is that we have to teach and what further ambitions we have with the part-time program. This is based on our insights about what we have to offer and on our ideas about what is needed and asked for. This constitutes a necessary starting point for our argument. But it may be desirable to redefine our agenda during the educational process as both our insights and those of our students develop.

Then we elaborate on why linking study with work practice and experience is necessary if our aims are to be realized. Our central thesis in this connection, however, is that sensible linking requires a preceding (and repeated) delinking. Therefore, we proceed with presenting some strategies for "delinking". With most of these we already have some experience, and if so, we will report on it. We also discuss a number of strategies for "relinking", which in practice are often interwoven with strategies for delinking.

Finally, we devote attention to problems related to the transference of new knowledge, insights and competences to real life practices. One key question in this connection is what responsibility MPA-programs have for supporting such transference.

The Mission of the
Erasmus University Part-Time PA Program

The part time PA program at Erasmus is set up for practitioners, professionals, having at least two years experience in a job in the public domain. It aims at teaching relevant PA knowledge and methods at an academic level in order to enhance professionalism, effectiveness and reflexivity of practitioners. In striving for these aims, the program tries to make a maximum use of the professional experience of the students and the real life setting they are working in daily. We elaborate on the main elements in this mission.

Public Administration Knowledge and Methods

Public Administration is about understanding the structure and functioning of the public sector, including all kind of agencies and private organizations performing public tasks. It is also about design, development, implementation and evaluation of policies and administrative or organizational arrangements or strategies in the public domain. For practitioners, Public Administration has to offer insight in processes and mechanisms that determine the functioning of public and semi-public bodies, their mutual interactions as well as interactions with societal organizations and citizens, intended or unintended outcomes of their policies or services. On the basis of these insights, Public Administration can contribute to new ways of analyzing, policy making and management, and hence to the professional performance of students.

Academic Education

The part-time program is education at an academic level. That means that students should not only have a clear image of the state of affairs in the public domain and be able to reproduce and apply Public Administration theory, but also to choose, criticize and develop different theoretical perspectives.

Professionalism and Effectiveness

Moreover, graduates should be able to relate, translate and apply Public Administration knowledge, insights and theory to real life practices and problems. Their repertoire of acting perspectives should be enlarged, their possibilities to choose between different perspectives improved. They should be able to present analyses and ideas in a convincing way, to advice, to collaborate and to manage. They should also be able to discuss and evaluate effectiveness of concrete policy and management measures and strategies.

Reflexivity

Finally, we want our students to become reflexive with respect to the sources and status of knowledge, societal and organizational problems, norms and values, and own roles and practices[3]. They should be aware of the epistemological nature and basis of knowledge and think about its implications for the status and utility of theories and research results. They should be critical on the definition of problems: whose definitions are they; are there other competing definitions; are other definitions possible? They should not take norms and values for granted, without recognizing them as such and without knowledge of the background of these normative ideas. Besides, they should be able to view and evaluate their own (professional) behavior from different perspectives.

Linking

These ambitions require that the content of the study and the related processes of learning and reflection be connected to the working practices of the students. This is, we think, self-evident for the third element. Professionalism and effectiveness as a matter of fact are explicitly dealing with transfer to real life practice. But our argument is that the other elements of our mission also need – or at least benefit from – a myriad of intelligent connections between study and work practice.

Acquiring factual knowledge of structure and functioning of public administration can be intensified and speeded up considerably if observing and experiencing public administration in practice supplement reading books and taking courses. In fact, most factual knowledge hardly needs to be presented. Also information on historical developments, trends, and theories can potentially be understood and positioned far easier and quicker by students with professional experience than by those without such experience. Experience and practice give "flesh and blood" to abstract notions and concepts.

Informed choice, critical review and sensible development of theories of Public Administration is also greatly facilitated, to say the least, if the relevant empirical reality is available. One could even claim that without the "resistance" that "reality" provides, a critical evaluation of theoretical notions is hardly possible.

Broader reflection on the meaning and impact of theories, of course, also needs "resistance" for thinking. But reflection on problem definitions, values and own behavior remains fairly abstract and without engagement, if it takes place outside the context to which it pertains. In our view, reflection, as does ethics, needs to be situated, that is to be related to concrete phenomena and issues.

This argument is a theory in itself. If we test this theory and reflect on it by confronting it with our own experience in the part time program, it appears to be a rather poor, if not invalid, one. For there is ample evidence that the mere existence of relevant work experience does not provide any guarantee for more effective and efficient professional and academic learning. On the contrary, it may considerably limit the speed and the quality of the process. This is so, we think, because socialization in real life practice tends to make this practice self-evident. Sometimes an exceptional student even thinks that Public Administration is about social work (being the domain in which he is working) and is initially simply not able to see other things that may be at stake in the public sphere. Far more general is the phenomenon that students have the conviction that they "know" the relevant reality. This is understandable since their "ideas" about the reality seem to be continuously confirmed by their perceived and interpreted experiences. This prevents recognizing the meaning and added value of insights and ideas an academic program can offer them. Theories tend to appear as intricate languages that scientists (should) use, but that only reformulate things already known. Theories may be judged according to the extent they correspond to the reality already known. But they hardly contribute to understanding that reality, leave alone to a different perspective on the same reality. In response to an assignment in which students were asked to apply a specified theoretical perspective to a known case, we received many papers in which students told their own story about the case and were convinced that they had fulfilled the assignment in an adequate way.

If real life practical experience has become self-evident, this severely limits critical reflection on theories and practices, development of new ideas and strategies, and their situated application. In fact we are often confronted with students with a fairly instrumental attitude. They know reality, its dynamics, its problems and they ask for the right (generic) solutions.

These experiences, and more specifically our interpretation of these, led to the conclusion that the constructive "linking" sketched above requires a preceding "delinking" process in which the self-evident nature of ideas and presuppositions about reality and its dynamics is removed. Acquiring and developing scientific knowledge requires that "common sense" be made debatable. Professionalization requires critical scrutiny of existing practices. Reflection requires distance. Therefore, we now turn to strategies for delinking in our part time MPA program.

Delinking

In this section we discuss strategies applied for delinking. Some of these strategies are translated into specific elements inserted in the study program. Other ones are strategies applied within most modules. Some strategies are applied more systematically than others. For some strategies we already have evidence as to their impact. If so, we will summarize these.

Presentation

Already in the presentation and marketing of the program, we are emphasizing that it is going to put question marks to things that appear to be self-evident. It is made clear that the program will provide much knowledge, theories and methods but that it will not result in recipes for success. It is an academic program training students to think, analyze, theorize, design, develop and evaluate themselves.

Interaction and Participation

Of course, listening to lectures, and reading books and articles can contribute to developing new ways of looking at things, and thus to reflection on own convictions and practices. But this process may be expected to be far more intensive if students are "forced" to deal with the material in a more active way. Therefore, we have introduced two elements in the program. The first is that we require students to actually attend the courses during two evenings a week. If they are absent more than incidentally, they usually get an additional assignment that requires them to engage actively in the subject matter. Second, we apply interactive forms of working, both between lecturer and students and amongst students. Thereby students are forced to make their ideas explicit and confront them in debate with other views from literature, lecturers or other students. Moreover they are forced to rethink these ideas, scrutinize indications for their validity and evaluate possible alternative views.

Our experience shows that practitioner students in general like the interactive mode very much. However, it does not always result in short term changes in the level of academic and reflective thinking. Discussions between the faculty and students on average seem to be more effective in this respect than debates among students. Group discussions without participation of the faculty tend to be valued less by students.

The Course "Explorations"

To clear the ground and give some direction for the critical and reflexive activity of students during the courses, the program starts with a course called "Explorations". In this module four key issues are discussed: structure and functions of government, societal problems and the role of government, public management and organization, and the added value of (Public Administration) science. With respect to each of these themes we begin with asking the students to define it, to formulate their norms, to express their observations on actual functioning and their presuppositions on the mechanisms behind it. Next, we ask further questions in a Socratic way to challenge their ideas and get at notions that are even more self-evident to students, but often appear to be debatable too. We explicitly identify different views among students and confront these with each other. The course is rather open ended with some conclusions, but also many questions and contradictory views and interpretations. Students are provided with an article on the theme to be studied before the next session, which starts with a presentation by a faculty member elaborating a specific view. After these two new inputs in the debate, students go into working groups and try to come up with counterarguments, which are then commented upon by the presenting faculty member.

Most students evaluate this module as "confusing". The things they were sure about appear not to be as self-evident as they thought they were. But at the same time they consider the module Explorations as very motivating. For the teaching faculty, that is the intended outcome. Students learn something else too. Knowledge is not offered to the student in a clear cut way. They have to look for it. And that knowledge can differ fundamentally from their "preconceived ideas".

In general, it certainly helps to "unfreeze", to delink students from key ideas that seemed to be self-evident.

Agenda Setting

At the end of the course "Explorations" students write an essay. In this paper they should formulate a substantive agenda for their study, starting from their own motivation on the one hand and the three most intriguing topics of the on the other. What do they want to learn, which questions do they want to answer during the study? By giving this assignment we force students to be explicit on what is new to them and on what they do not know or understand. This is meant as a way to consolidate the uneasiness induced in Explorations. Still, reading the essays, we must conclude that many students redefine fundamental questions in fairly instrumental ones. The process of delinking and unfreezing is not a one shot business.

Uncommon Interpretations

In the different courses many real life cases, sometimes directly from students' experiences, are discussed. One function of this practice is to train students in assessing and reflecting on the nature of the situation or problem or trend. It appears that often students come up with a straightforward interpretation. They experience the situation as the observation of simple facts. By offering them alternative perspectives and interpretations, explicitly using theoretical notions or not, we show that on scrutiny many things are not as self-evident as they seem. It often appears to require much persistence and supervision to force students to actually apply different perspectives and evaluate these.

Feed-back

In papers and presentations, students give their account of specific situations and processes, again often from their own practice. This provides us with extra opportunities to give feedback. Not only in terms of the (in)validity of the account per se, but also in terms of the quality of the evidence and arguments to support it. Thus, in so far available time allows us to do so; we not only mark papers, but also give students qualitative comments in written or oral form.

Mentors

Immediately after the introductory module "Explorations", students are asked to complete a self-assessment of their competences with respect to study, research, communication, consultancy and management. If desirable they are then linked to a faculty member who acts as a mentor. In consultation between student and mentor a plan is formulated to improve relevant competences. Sometimes this plan includes a specific task to be performed in certain modules (presentation, writing, analytical skills, research methods) or taking additional courses. It is also possible that the plan includes exercises or experiments to be done in the own work practice. In this case students are forced to act in new ways in known situations and learn, by consequence, to view these situations in new terms. Moreover, the consultations between mentor and students on all kind of aspects of the study and real life practice may contribute to "delinking".

At this moment, however, we do not have much evidence on the impact of mentorships in this respect. Nevertheless, on the basis of our first impressions, we are looking for possibilities to improve the effectiveness of this part of the program.

Collaboration

Another device for delinking is situated in the interaction between students. If they have to work together in small groups on projects, cases or papers, or in group discussions, their – different – views and experiences are confronted with each other. This is especially the case if the groups are heterogeneous in terms of tasks and functions the members fulfill in their jobs, and in terms of the (policy) areas they work in. We require students to work with different partners on different assignments to be done during the study, thus inducing more diverse interaction and confrontation of ideas. That also prevents them to focus on the things they are already good at, leaving their weaker competences to their fellow-students.

Start Session Master's Year

In the modules of the Master's year the emphasis is on reflection, which by definition implies an element of delinking. As part of a two-day starting session of the Master's year, we conduct a social simulation experiment in which students occupy different administrative positions. In this way we create a collective "reality", thus enabling joint reflection. This is done in an evaluative session after the simulation. It appears that – even after one year study in which the preceding "delinking" instruments were applied – it is fairly difficult to organize "distance" to what is going on in the simulation while it is played. However, in the evaluative sessions such distance is quite well realized (probably due to skills students had acquired in the mean time), thus enabling thoughtful reflection on how patterns and self-evident notions are generated and consolidated and on conditions and strategies for change.

Reflexive Modules in the Master's Year

In the thematic modules of the Master's year, we try to create the conditions for more reflection, both on theories and practices. There are four modules in the Master's year:
–   policy and society;
–   governance and the public sector;
–   public management and organizational change;
–   the Public Administration professional.

In these modules, the emphasis is on debate and on assessment of societal, administrative and organizational problems, on the meaning and usefulness of theoretical approaches, on the construction of strategies and solutions, as well as on the arguments on which these are founded.[4] All these elements, however, require self-evidences to be put at issue. It continues to be the task of the faculty to do this. In this part of the program we try to stimulate reflection by the student even more than before.

Relinking

Delinking enables relinking in new ways, thus bringing home the added value of the program, not only in an academic sense but also in a professional mode. To be sure, relinking is already embedded to a considerable extent in the devices we designed to delink. For example, tempting students to look with new lenses to known situations is at the same time delinking and relinking. Things cannot simply be taken for what they seem to be. But also: new theoretical perspectives can be applied in sensible ways. Or: perspectives from other actors make sense as well.

Still, it is useful to make an analytic distinction between delinking and relinking and summarize the main instruments we use for the latter. This is so because assessing the quality of the program and developing it further, requires that delinking and relinking be evaluated each on its own account. For if there is much delinking while there effectively is no relinking, the net result with respect to our mission is too meager. Moreover some devices have actually more to offer with respect to relinking than to delinking.

Again: Interaction and Participation

Sensible linking of new perspectives and theoretical ideas to real life practice is only possible if students engage in applying them actively in a critical mode. The latter aspect is enhanced by debate among students and between students and faculty on the applicability and implications of perspectives, concepts, and presupposed relations. In fact, such debates constitute the core element of the reflective modules in the Master's year. The following instruments for relinking (except the last one) are already applied in their first year.

Examples From Work Practice

An obvious device is illustrating analysis and theories presented in courses by examples that are recognizable for most, if not all students. Through earlier occupations or administrative functions, research and consulting, our faculty is able to produce such examples. It's our observation that this is not only illuminating for the students, but also motivating to follow the line and consequences of the argument.

Assignments with Respect to Work Practice

One step further, in fact combining both previous devices, is forcing students to apply perspectives and ideas studied to real life cases. In early stages of the program it seems wise to choose cases that are recognizable, but not very familiar to students. Thus they learn linking without too much interference of existing links (self-evidences). Gradually, it should be possible to come closer to the own working practice in new ways. Of course, feed-back on such assignments is vital in order to guide the process of relinking.

Guest Speakers

Another way to (re)link insights from the study to actual practice is the invitation of and debate with guest speakers, themselves practitioners or consultants. They present theories, analyses and practices they use in their profession, which may provide students new practical ideas and insights. Apart from that a debate with a guest speaker is a way to explore, test and support (or reject) notions and ideas acquired during the study. It also offers a possibility for our part-time students to improve their interview skills by trying to discover what relevant questions could be asked. The guest is in that case not giving a lecture, but is requested to answer questions.

It is clear from our experience that guest speakers should be carefully selected. They should be able to be concrete and reflexive at the same time. That is, his or her contribution should be "empirical" and recognizable and leave room for differences in interpretation and discussion. We also found that it is necessary that guest speakers are properly embedded in the course. That is, the faculty running the course must make clear for what purpose the guest is invited and what kind of discussion with the guest will be useful. Moreover, during or after the session the faculty should pick up main points from the presentation and debate in order to explicitly connect them with the theme of the course and theoretical notions considered. Like in the case of practice related assignments, the (re)linking process should (especially in early stages of the program) not be fully left to the students.

Collaboration

After training in delinking and having digested Public Administration theories and approaches, relinking may be facilitated by collaboration between students. They will discuss how such relinking might sensibly get shape. Contrary to the heterogeneous groups that we use for delinking, it seems useful here to work with homogeneous groups. Students working in the same (type of) organization then search in mutual exchange for new interpretations and analyses of what is going on (or how things might be changed) in own practices, utilizing what is learned during the study. Such debate actually is about *how* new links can be made.

Final Project

In the final project of the Master's year – which can have different formats – relinking is the core business. Students investigate a specific issue or case and prepare a research report, a policy advice or an organizational analysis and advice. They should utilize Public Administration theory in dealing with empirical phenomena and specific policy or management problems. Frequently, students engage in a project directly related to their daily work, in many cases devoted to an issue or problem with which their own organization is struggling. In such cases the task of the student and his/her supervisor is to keep organizing distance (delinking) while at the same time making sound and solid new links between theory and practice, not only in the analysis, but also in designing plans and strategies, and eventually in their implementation.

Transference

Finally, an additional problem of relating study to work practice should be addressed. However, successful the program is in delinking and relinking thoughts, knowledge and insight at the level of the individual student, transference of this new skills and competence to actual professional behavior, is dependent on situational factors and mechanisms The point is that professional behavior is also social and organizational behavior. It is not only subject to professional expertise and methods, but also to social codes and expectations. Especially with respect to "reflection" in general and "unconventional" interpretations and solutions specifically, individual professionals are not always able to "realize" these in an uncomprehending environment. In fact the problem becomes: how to delink, change and relink thoughts and ideas in others. This problem should get due attention in our program. We might devote some time and energy in the module on the Public Administration Professional to make students aware of the problem and to reflect on what can be done about it. In a sense the final project – if this is connected to the daily work practice – can be considered as an exercise in transference to organizational behavior.

It is an interesting question whether the program and the university have a duty to fulfill in this respect after students have completed their study. And if so, how.

Results

The results of our educational strategy thus far are mixed. In general, students are fairly satisfied with the program. They often report that it helps to view their own situations and work in new ways and consequently to act in new modes. Many students also report that the program influences their way of thinking and it generates new questions. This is also substantiated by essays students write in the framework of the final module of the program. In this assignment they are asked to return to their initial expectations and agenda, as formulated in an essay in the first module, and to reflect on what they have learned in the mean time.

On the other hand we observe that graduates differ widely in the extent to which they are able to reflect, analyze critically and theorize upon policy, administrative and organizational issues.

Conclusion

In this paper we argued that an MPA-program that seeks to combine academic education, practice oriented professionalization and reflexivity has much to gain from linking study and work practice. We also identified the pitfalls of the lack of distance practitioners often have from their practice and day-to-day experience. Therefore, we concluded that a major investment in "delinking" has to be made. Students can be too close to the subject they like to study. New sensible connections have to be established between what is learned and elaborated during the study and that very practice part time student's experience everyday.

A number of instruments we thought of and applied until now, enhanced both steps of delinking and relinking. We outlined how we expect and experienced the last years them to work. But this is only a set of first steps. We have much to learn from pedagogical literature and from the experiences of others who manage programs for practitioners. We are now in a position to (re)link such insights and experiences to our own day-to-day practice in the program. This is a consequence of the reformulation of the pedagogical problem that is central to programs like Public Administration and Public Affairs.

What we aim for is that students have the experience that the great poet T.S. Elliot once phrased so wonderfully:

> *We shall not cease from exploration*
> *And the end of all our exploring*
> *Will be to arrive where we started*
> *And know the place for the first time.*

Endnotes

[1] Weiss, C.H. and M.J. Bucuvalas (1980). Social Science Research and Decision Making. New York, Guildford, Colombia University Press; Lindblom, C.E. and D.K. Cohen (1979). Usable Knowledge: social change and social problem solving. New Haven, Yale University Press; Ringeling, A.B. (1983). De instrumenten van het beleid (The Instruments of Public Policy) inaugural lecture, Erasmus Universiteit Rotterdam, Alphen aan de Rijn, Samsom.

[2] These questions focus on the supply side. Of course, similar questions can be asked about the demand side, but these are beyond the scope of this contribution.

[3] See Van der Meer, F.B. (2008). Organizing reflectivity, paper MPA Pedagogical Workshop, Limerick.

[4] Schön, D.A. (1983.) The Reflective Practitioner: how professionals think in action. New York: Basic Books.

6

The implementation of the Bologna Process in France: Existing Paradoxes and Remaining Obstacles

Laure Castin

Much has been said already about the Bologna Process. It could, however, be useful to point out some paradoxes especially in regard to the peculiarities of its implementation in the French Higher Education landscape.

It has first to be reminded that the Bologna Process is an intergovernmental European reform process, it's a collective awareness and a collective answer to the challenges of the global society.

In the 1980s, the governments in Europe became aware that it was urgently needed to reform the European Higher Education Area because the 4000 European higher education institutions couldn't respond effectively to the challenges of the global society: they were unable to compete with bigger American and Asiatic universities, unable to keep young researchers from moving to other more attractive countries; they were badly represented on the international stage and did not have enough funds.[1]

To this collective challenge, was foreseen a collective answer. The main purpose of the Bologna process was and still remains to develop a European Higher Education Area in 2010 "based on institutional autonomy, academic freedom, equal opportunities and democratic principles, respect of the European cultural diversity that will facilitate mobility, increase employability and strengthen Europe's attractiveness and competitiveness".[2] The main idea was thus to create an open space where students, graduates and higher education staff could benefit from unhampered mobility and equitable access to high quality higher education through mutual recognition of any degrees, transparency (readable and comparable degrees organised in a three-cycle-structure) and cooperation in quality assurance.

Although set in motion in 1999, the reform of the European Higher Education Area is undoubtedly linked to the strategic trends of the Lisbon Agenda (2000): becoming a leading European global and knowledge-based economy requires indeed to reform the educational system thus education plays a key role in defining and transmitting the values on which each society is built.

The main purpose of the Bologna process represents also a big paradox when being replaced in the framework of the Lisbon Agenda: its underlying values are solidarity, equal opportunities, mutual trust and understanding, partnerships among the universities, but in the global competitive context, which means that European universities will have to compete between themselves. Globalization indeed means enhancing research and training excellence: far away from the Bologna principles of solidarity and cooperation. The instruments of the Bologna Process in favour of mobility, academic recognition and training will undoubtedly oblige universities to be more and more attractive and thus they will lead to increasing competition between themselves.

These obvious paradoxes of the Bologna Process compared to the requirements of the Lisbon Agenda are still not really dealt with on the political level.

The Ministers responsible for Higher Education in the countries participating in the Bologna process reviewed the progress made in a big meeting in London in May 2007. At the end of the meeting, they published a communiqué and underlined the importance of "having strong institutions which are diverse, in favour of non-discrimination and equitable access throughout the EHEA". They valued European diversity, rejecting the idea of having a standard system all over Europe and enhanced the commitment to increase the compatibility and comparability of the higher education systems.[3]

In the London communiqué as well, was underlined the need of having strong institutions of higher education, which are adequately funded, autonomous and accountable. It was pointed out that the real reforms were still to be done: increasing budget dedicated to education and research (public and private), autonomy of the higher education institutions, better quality of study period and better quality of ingoing mobility. But no word was said about ineluctable competitiveness between universities on the European stage.

France is currently facing these paradoxes of the Bologna Process with the implementation of the reform of its universities. Adopted in August 2007, the law *Libertés et Responsabilités des Universités* (LRU) could be directly linked with the London Communiqué of the Bologna Process because its main purpose is to transfer to French universities budget and management autonomy.[4] These measures complete the current restructuring of the French Higher Education space launched with the creation in 2006 of Research and Higher Education Centres (*Pôles de recherche et d'enseignement supérieur - PRES*).[5] Public or private, research or higher education institutions or organisations (such as Universities and *grandes écoles* for instance) are invited to work closer or even to merge to put an end to the territorial splitting up of higher education and research centres in France. They are invited to pool their activities and resources to reach a genuine critical mass, identify strong education and research competencies to become more attractive on the international level.[6]

A great deal of universities in France, if not all of them, is strongly in favour of a structural reform. A specificity of the French Higher Education system till now is the dualism between universities and *grandes écoles* and it has largely contributed to put the first at a disadvantage. While universities provide education and training for large student numbers and have an obligation of open access since the 1960s,[7] *grandes écoles* are highly selective and offer training for the future elite in the state and in industry. But only universities and national research centres (like the CNRS) are dedicated to research activities.[8]

Going into a closer cooperation or into a merging process could therefore help the lines blur in the French traditional dualist system.

If French universities give support to a structural reform, they however totally disagree with the idea suggested by President Sarkozy in July 2007 to give them the choice to implement the reform now or within five years. They recommend a collective move towards the reform and reject the idea of a "*deux vitesses* system".

At the same time, French universities are against the idea of increasing tuition fees and against the idea of selection access to the first cycle (Bachelor's degree). These reactions are stressing the remaining effects of the massified higher education from the 1960s, and of the equality policy carried out towards the universities in a centralized state.

But it has to be faced that implementing structural reforms will set universities in competition on the national level. It could be said that the competition has already started with the creation of the Research and Higher Education Centres. The idea supported by the Attali report to President Sarkozy in January 2008 to allow ten future centres of excellence in training and research to be financed up to 80% by private fundraising[9] goes into the same direction. Few words have been said about that till now although everybody is perfectly aware of the implications of these structural reforms. French universities are currently living through a transitional and historical period of time.

Reforming French universities in the framework of the Bologna Process is not only a matter of budget and management autonomy or a matter linked to the creation of PRES. For many years, it concerns all aspects of the universities'activities but strong efforts have still to be done to increase legibility, transferability and transparency. The Bologna Process is still facing obstacles in France.

Systematic implementation of the three-cycle system (LMD system standing for Licence-Master-Doctorate or the so called 3-5-8 system) has started in 2002 in the universities (except in the health sector). *Grandes écoles* have so far remained largely untouched by the reforms.[10] The move to the LMD system goes hand in hand with the consequent implementation of modularisation, and the move to a semester system. Part of modularisation means the higher education establishments have had to define a competence-based learning system (learning outcomes).

There is a slow ongoing move towards student-centred higher education and away from teacher driven provision: the curricula reform leads to qualifications better suited both to the needs of the labour market and to further study. The policy encouraged by the National Ministry of Education in terms of tracks and flexible learning paths or transition paths between different tracks leading to certain specialisation aims at improving student orientation in the first years and making clearer the competences of graduates.

But there is still a strong resistance among professors and lecturers. In the framework of LMD reform, they have created a great amount of bachelor or master degrees without taking the needs of the students and labour market enough into account. Efforts have still to be done in the future in implementing European Credit Transfer based on learning outcomes and student workload. That's the only way to fair recognition of higher education qualifications, periods of study and prior learning. Because easily readable and comparable degrees and accessible information on educational systems and qualification frameworks are necessary for students mobility. And mobility of students, staff and lecturers/researchers is one of the core elements of the Bologna Process.

No need to stress student's mobility creates opportunities for personal growth, develop first step cooperation between individuals and institutions, enhance the quality of higher education and research. But it remains difficult to organize mobility between European universities.

Enhancing international mobility is an overarching political objective laid down in the annual Colloquium of the French University Rectors' Conference (CPU) in Nantes, 15-17 March 2006. The intention is to replace mobility largely founded on historical (French speaking countries) and economical reasons by contracted mobility within a pedagogical exchange policy. Another objective is to encourage international mobility of French students and thirdly to facilitate mobility within France based on the LMD system.[11]

Four main achievements have recently been made to foster France's contribution to the creation of the European Higher Education Area:[12]

– Evolution of the legislation about the award of degrees within international partnerships (joint degree in particular) with the decree

n° 2005-450 dated 11 May 2005. The building up of a competitive European Higher Education Area requires the development of partnerships between universities from several countries so as to design common training courses and to award widely recognized joint degree.
- Generalization of the LMD Reform.
- New organisation of doctoral schools and doctoral programmes (decrees dated 25 April 2002 and 7 August 2006) according to the Salzburg 10 points Quality program in 2005. The international joint supervision of doctoral thesis is as well encouraged.
- A completely revised French system for the assessment of research and higher education quality with the creation of a new Agency, Agence pour l'évaluation de la recherche et de l'enseignement supérieur - AERES set in motion in 2007.

Although all these measures have been taken to remove obstacles to ingoing or outgoing student mobility, there is still a lot to do to improve mobility, quality, and academic recognition. But more important is, maybe, to be plainly aware of the competition consequences of the ongoing structural reform. The big work ahead is indeed to favour a more efficient university governance, to strengthen autonomy, to improve funding through taking better account of their actions and outcomes. Equality policy is over. To cope with that requires a totally new universitary culture and state of mind in France. It's only the first big challenge France's universities have to face nowadays in this transitional and historical period of time, because in our highly changing world, there will be a continuing need to adapt our higher education systems, to ensure that the European Higher Education Area remains competitive and can respond effectively to the challenges of global society.

Endnotes

[1] Whereas the USA dedicated 2.6 % of the national budget to education and research, the European Union only allowed 1,1 % of the national budget to these matters.

[2] London Communiqué, "Towards the European Higher Education Area: responding to challenges in a globalised world", 18 May 2007, p.1.

[3] Ibid., p.1.

[4] Loi n°2007-1199 du 10 août 2007 relative aux libertés et responsabilités des universités (LRU).

[5] The PRES represents one of the new cooperation tools in the French legislation (*Loi de programme pour la recherche* du 18 avril 2006). The first report on the impact of such a restructuring was published by the French *Inspection générale de l'administration et de l'éducation nationale* (IGAENR) in September 2007, see the report 2007-079 "La mise en place des pôles de recherche et d'enseignement supérieur" by Jean-Richard Cytermann, website: http://www.education.gouv.fr/cid5690/mise-en-place-des-poles-de-recherche-et-d-enseignement-superieur-pres.html. See as well the report by Attali to President Sarkozy (from the *Commission pour la libération de la croissance française*), published in Le Monde, 21 January 2008, p.1 and 8: the report favors the creation of "10 pôles d'excellence", 10 French centers of excellence in research and education, financed up to 80 % by private fund-raising.

[6] 9 centres have already officially been created when others are still negociating their future cooperation modalities. It has to be precised that some are involved in a merging process whereas the others prefer to enhance a strong cooperation in their activities.

[7] In the 1960s, all the systems of higher education in Europe were affected by a prominent and striking increase in social demand which led in France to the introduction of a completely open-door system, abolishing any kind of selection between the secondary school and university. University structure and curricula remained however unchanged, unable to cope with the social diversity and needs of new generations of students. As a result, the number of university dropouts increased substantially and the output of high education establishments had little to do with the evolution and requirements of the labour market. The same happened in Italy, see R.Moscati, "The implementation of the Bologna Process in Italy", text deriving in part from an essay included in the *2006 International Handbook of Higher Education.*

[8] Governance structures differ greatly between the two systems: universities come under the authority of the national ministry of education's director-

ate of higher education whereas *grandes écoles* fall under the authority of various public authorities, with a prominent presence of industrial stakeholders, see "The extent and impact of higher education curricular reform across Europe", Final Report to the Directorate-General for Education and Culture of the European Commission, 2006, pp. 67-68.

[9] See the Report by Attali to President Sarkozy, *op.cit.*, pp.1 and 8.

[10] Like universities however, they are entitled to award master degrees to their graduates (in the framework of an accreditation process according to state procedure and criteria).

[11] See "The extent and impact of higher education curricular reform across Europe", *op.cit.*, pp. 67-68.

[12] For more details, see the National Report for France – Bologna Process 2005-2007 from the Directorate General for Higher Education - DGES, Ministère de l'Education nationale, de l'enseignement supérieur et de la recherche, December 2006, 21p.

Universities and Wealth Creation
in Economic Regions

7

Rethinking the Role of the University for the Entrepreneurial Society

David B. Audretsch

Introduction

Globalization has had a profound impact on a broad spectrum of issues confronting public policy. The purpose of this chapter is to examine how the role of the university in society is being impacted by globalization. The second section of the paper reviews the traditional role of the university in what has been called the era of the managed economy, or when the factor of physical capital was the engine of economic growth, employment and competitiveness. The third section of the paper explains how and why globalization rendered the public policy framework – the managed economy – ineffective and how a new framework, the entrepreneurial society is replacing it. The fourth section examines how the role of the university is evolving in the entrepreneurial society. A summary and conclusion are provided in the final section.

The University in the Managed Economy

In the managed economy of the 1950s and early1960s, the university made significant contributions to not just the most fundamental social and political values of America, but also of western civilization. The American universities by the twentieth century had evolved from being extensions of religious institutions to being proud and independent institutions of higher learning in the Humboldt tradition. Humboldt had been a giant of a scholar and statesman in Berlin during the early 1800s. He shaped a new tradition for universities, with freedom of thought, learning, intellectual exchange, research and scholarship as the cornerstone of the university. As the Humboldt tradition diffused first throughout Europe and later the United States, it had a profound impact on universities. They broke free of parochial chains inherent in championing a non-secular view to becoming committed first and foremost to a fierce independence in thinking, learning, scholarship and research. Such independence in thought and inquiry is, of course, a value deeply at the heart of America, if not western civilization. Thus, throughout Europe and certainly the United States, the university emerged in the twentieth century as an institution essential to the values requisite to a democratic and free society. The university was a place where young people learned to think freely and independently, and became prepared as the next generation progulamating those values underlying at least the western view of what constitutes a humane and civilized society.

But to say that the Humboldt University, or rather America's newer and more modern and certainly Americanized version of the Humboldt University, served a great social and political contribution is not to say that it was considered to be of significant economic relevance. The university was important to create well-rounded, reflective and thoughtful citizens, equipped with the requisite appreciation of western civilization and learning but also respect for independence of thinking and inquiry, to ensure the basis of a democratic society. The western, Humboldt University was obviously at odds with a totalitarianism society. In the communist and totalitarian revolutions, perhaps the first and foremost target, other than the Czar, was the university and its professors. If you controlled the freedom to think, you might be able to control society. Thus, the freedom of thinking and inquiry that served as the foundation of the Humboldt University was not coincidentally also the foundation of a free society.

When Berlin was divided into sectors reflecting the victories allies at the Potsdam Conference following the Second World War, the major university, named after Humboldt, the Humboldt University was located in the Russian Sector in the eastern sector of Berlin. One of the early steps taken by the Russians and her East German communist allies was to quickly dismantle the freedom of professors at the Humboldt University and place them under increased restrictions, monitoring and controls. Ironically, the Humboldt University was no longer a university in the Humboldt tradition. It is also surely no coincidence that one of the first and most significant steps taken by the United States in response to the dismantling, or rather, the new restrictions imposed on expression, scholarly exchange and research at the then communist Humboldt University, was to create a new university in West Berlin, aptly named The Free University of Berlin. This new university in the west, created by a massive injection of funds, resources and goodwill from the United States, presented a striking contrast to her famous but emasculated counterpart in then communist controlled East Berlin. As its name reflected, thinking, expression, scholarly pursuit and research was first and foremost *free*. It was widely deemed as essential that such a free university serve as a beacon but also a catalyst for a free democratic society in allied occupied West Berlin. Some thirty years later, with the fall of the Berlin Wall, it was the Humboldt University that underwent a fundamental transformation and became like the Free University of Berlin, and not *vice versa*. Just as a controlled and restricted university was essential in the totalitarian communist regime of post-war East Germany, so free and unrestricted universities are a cornerstone of democracies.

But to say that the university made an essential contribution to social and democratic principles is not to say that it also made a positive economic contribution. In fact, during the post-war era characterized by the capital-driven managed economy, the university was generally seen as an economic drain or at best neutral to the economy. As chapter three points out, the Nobel-prize winning Solow Model in economics put the emphasis on economic growth directly on two factors, physical capital and labor that would go into factories to work with that capital. What could the university contribute to these factors? Surely, investing resources in the university contributed little to investments in physical plants, machines and equipment used for production. Rather, funds used to finance university education and research seemed to many like a diversion from the real business of doing business in the real world. Similarly, what was needed to make factories work were laborers who were beyond anything obedient, reliable, had total allegiance to the rules and did what they were told.

Thus, in the managed economy of the 1950s and early 1960s, the university undoubtedly made a valuable contribution to society in terms of passing on the values of civilization and democracy, but few felt that the university had much to contribute as an engine of economic growth. In fact, the opposite was true; the university was typically viewed as a cost to be incurred for making sure that the cultural and democratic foundations underlying society prospered.

The Emergence of the Entrepreneurial Society

When the Berlin Wall fell in November 1989, most scholars, as well as policy makers, anticipated what was expressed as a peace dividend for Europe in terms of economic growth. After all, the post-war recovery of Europe, and especially particular countries such as Germany and Sweden, had been based on wresting the comparative advantage from the United States in key capital-based industries, such as automobiles, steel, and machine tools. Economic growth, employment and competitiveness throughout the post-war era had been driven by physical capital. Just as Robert Solow[1,2] was awarded a Nobel Prize for identifying physical capital as the main factor driving economic growth that could be identified, it was surely no coincidence that decades earlier Karl Marx had titled his history changing book *Kapital*.

It came as something of a shock when it became clear that, rather than reinforce the post-war European comparative advantage in capital-goods industries, the post-Berlin Wall globalization triggered a loss in European competitiveness in its stalwart traditional manufacturing industries. Driven by the harsh logic of globalization, new, European companies were increasingly choosing to outsource and offshore in a desperate effort to remain competitive. While this might have preserved, or even enhanced, the competitiveness of some European companies, it eroded the levels of economic growth throughout Europe and triggered increases in unemployment that retched upwards throughout the decade of the 1990s.

For example, there were about ten million people employed in manufacturing jobs in Germany in 1990. By 2005, this number had fallen to 7.5 million. Nearly one-quarter of the jobs were in manufacturing when the decade began; 15 years later only one-fifth of employment was in manufacturing. Over this same period, unemployment doubled, from 5 percent to double digits.

Even as the comparative advantage in (physical) capital in Europe was beginning to fade, scholars and policy makers began to recognize the primacy of a very different factor of production – knowledge capital, which is based not just on technological and scientific knowledge, but also in a broader sense of ideas, creativity, originality and novelty. The recognition by Romer,[3] and Lucas,[4] among others, that knowledge was not only endogenous, but that it also spilled over for commercialization by firms and individuals other than the firm or university actually creating that knowledge in the first place, shifted the policy debate and focus away from instruments inducing investments in physical capital towards instruments generating knowledge and ideas, such as university research, education and training, and patents.

Thus, even as Europe began losing the comparativeness advantage in physical capital, it seemed to be at least as well poised to thrive with a knowledge-based economy. In particularly, the Nordic countries, but also Northern Europe more generally, ranked among the world's leaders in terms of the most common measures of knowledge. Thus, the inability of countries which were knowledge leaders, such as Sweden, to prosper in the global economy was so striking that it was referred to as the Swedish Paradox. However, it was not just Sweden that exhibited surprising low growth rates and rising unemployment; while at the same time have high rates of investment in research, human capital and culture. The European Union adapted the label to describe what it termed as *the European Paradox*. While the prescriptions of investments in knowledge generated economic models of scholars, the experience of Sweden, and in fact much of Europe, was suggesting that the links between knowledge and growth are, in fact, more nuanced and complicated.

The conditions inherent in knowledge – high uncertainty, asymmetries and transactions cost – result in decision making hierarchies in companies reaching the decision not to pursue and try to commercialize new ideas that individual economic agents, or groups or teams of economic agents think are potentially valuable and should be pursued. The characteristics of knowledge distinguishing it from information, a high degree of uncertainty combined with non-trivial asymmetries, combined with a broad spectrum of institutions, rules and regulations impose what Audretsch et al. (2006) term *the knowledge filter*. The knowledge filter is the gap between knowledge that has a potential commercial value and knowledge that is actually commercialized. The greater is the knowledge filter, the more pronounced is the gap between new knowledge and commercialized knowledge.

It is the knowledge filter that impedes investments in knowledge from spilling over for commercialization that leads to the so-called Swedish Paradox and European Paradox. Europe was not alone in having investments in knowledge choked off from resulting in economic growth by the knowledge filter. The United States has also not been able to avoid the knowledge filter. In fact, the knowledge filter impeding the commercialization of investments in research and knowledge can be formidable. As Senator Birch Bayh warned, "A wealth of scientific talent at American colleges and universities – talent responsible for the development of numerous innovative scientific breakthroughs each year – is going to waste as a result of bureaucratic red tape and illogical government regulations...."[5] It is the knowledge filter that stands between investment in research on the one hand, and its commercialization through innovation, leading ultimately to economic growth, on the other.

Seen through the eyes of Senator Bayh, the magnitude of the knowledge filter is daunting, "What sense does it make to spend billions of dollars each year on government-supported research and then prevent new developments from benefiting the American people because of dumb bureaucratic red tape?"[6]

Confronted with what is termed the knowledge impeding the spillover of knowledge from the firm or organization where it was originally generated, for commercialization by third-party firms, public policy instruments to promote investment in knowledge, such human capital, R&D, and university research may not adequately generate economic growth. One interpretation of the *European Paradox*, where such investments in new knowledge have certainly been substantial and sustained, but vigorous growth and reduction of unemployment have remained elusive, is that the presence of such an imposing knowledge filter chokes off the commercialization of those new knowledge investments, resulting in diminished innovative activity and ultimately stagnant growth.

By choking off the spillover and commercialization of knowledge and new ideas, the knowledge filter at the same time presents opportunities for individuals, or teams of individuals, that might place a high valuation on the potential of that knowledge, to become entrepreneurs. If people are not able to pursue and implement their ideas and vision within the context of an incumbent firm or organization, in order to appropriate the value of her knowledge and ideas, the agent would need to start a new firm, which is to become an entrepreneur.

The entrepreneurial startup reflects knowledge spillover entrepreneurship because the ideas serving as the basis for the startup were obtained, typically for little or no cost, from a different, incumbent firm or organization. Thus, knowledge spillover entrepreneurship serves as a conduit for new ideas generated created by an incumbent organization but otherwise left uncommercialized to spillover.

The knowledge spillover theory of entrepreneurship[7] suggests that contexts which are rich in knowledge will tend to generate more entrepreneurial opportunities. Fewer entrepreneurial opportunities will be generated in a context with a lower amount of investment in new ideas and knowledge. By contrast, those contexts that have less knowledge will generate fewer entrepreneurial opportunities. A consequence of globalization, which has shifted the comparative advantage of developed countries from physical capital to knowledge capital, is that entrepreneurial opportunities become more pervasive.[8]

The Entrepreneurial University

The shift in comparative advantage away from the capital intensity of the smokestack-based economy suggests a rethinking of policy to promote growth, jobs, and competitiveness. Sources of knowledge, ideas, and creativity become the focus of policy. One important source of knowledge is the university. When competitiveness was based on smokestacks, the university made important social, political, and cultural contributions but little in the economic realm. However, as competitiveness becomes dependent upon knowledge, ideas, and creativity, the university emerges as crucial for economic growth.[9]

Figure 1: The Entrepreneurial University

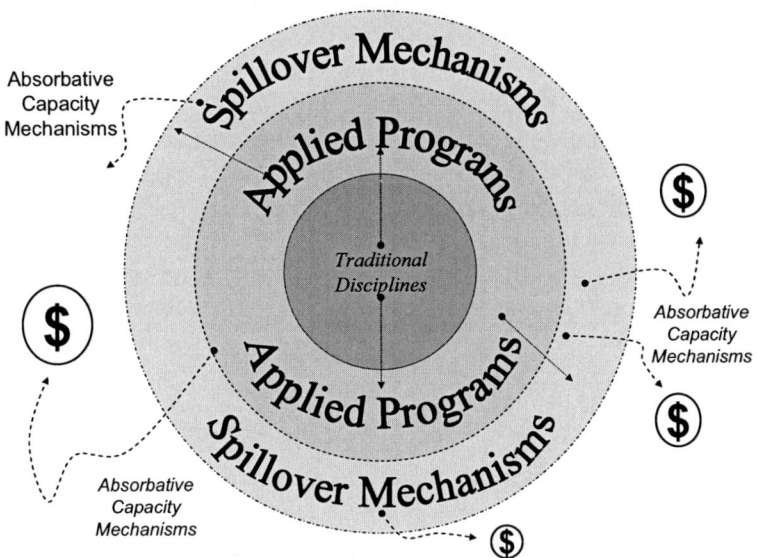

One important contribution the university makes is in generating new ideas and knowledge in the basic disciplines, which is the traditional core of the university. These disciplines represented the core of the traditional Humboldt model of the university,[10] which was proudly free from both church and government influence. In the Humboldt core of the university, shown in the center of Figure 1, knowledge is valued for its own sake, with little thought or consideration for its applicability in the "real world." However, as the demand for real world applications of this knowledge has increased over time, applied and professional programs have been created. Examples of such applied programs, depicted by the second circle in Figure 1, include business schools, informatics, health, education, bioengineering, and public policy.

The land-grant universities in the U.S. are a deviation from the Humboldt model.[11] The Morrill Act, more commonly known as the Land Grant Act, was signed into law by Abraham Lincoln in 1862. The Act granted each state land that was to be used in perpetuity to fund agricultural and mechanical colleges benefiting the state.[12] The idea was to offer the opportunity for higher education to the members of the working class and not just those destined to religious or contemplative professions. Thus, the United States has a long and rich tradition, at least at the land grant universities, of offering not just basic research and knowledge but also applied programs as well, particularly in agriculture.

A crucial distinction between these applied programs and fields and the basic disciplines is the orientation of the former to making a contribution to society beyond the walls surrounding the ivory tower in the inner circle of Figure 1. Without interest and demand for these fields from outside the university, they would not be sustainable over time. In fact, their development and evolution is typically shaped by societal needs and interests. By contrast, the development and evolution of the basic disciplines tends to be shaped and influenced by the disciplines themselves, i.e. *knowledge for its own sake.*

However, even the addition of applied research and professional education does not suffice in generating sufficient spillovers from the knowledge source, the university, to commercialized innovations generating growth in the regional and state economies. Investments in the two inner circles of Figure 1 alone do not suffice. In an effort to penetrate the knowledge filter and facilitate the spillover of university-generated knowledge and ideas, a third layer has been developed at universities, which represents mechanisms for transferring university-created technology and knowledge, such as offices of technology, incubators, and university-based research parks. The goal of these university-based offices and mechanisms is to serve as conduits facilitating the spillover of knowledge from the inner two circles representing basic and applied knowledge and the external economy, typically in the region or state.

The ability of a region to absorb university-based knowledge also contributes to the effectiveness of university spillovers. Such absorptive capacity mechanisms exist outside of the university and include the existence of complementary research-oriented large and small firms, non-profit organizations with a mandate to generate links between the regional economy and the university, and a rich set of entrepreneurial networks constituting the basis for vibrant entrepreneurship capital. Such external mechanisms ensure not only that knowledge spillovers will occur, but that they also will tend to be localized within the region that invested in creating that knowledge in the first place. Regional absorptive capacity is the mechanism facilitating the localized appropriation of knowledge spillovers.

There are compelling reasons to conjecture that the contribution of public policy support may actually be greater in regions that already have some of the knowledge and human capital assets, but knowledge spillovers and successful commercialization, along with science-based entrepreneurship, is limited as a result of the four fundamental sources of market and/or locational failure impeding high technology entrepreneurship – network externalities, knowledge externalities, learning externalities, and demonstration externalities.

Network externalities result from the value of an individual's or firm's capabilities being conditional upon the geographic proximity of complementary firms and individuals. Local proximity is essential for accessing these complementary inputs. This makes the value of an entrepreneurial firm greater in the (local) presence of other entrepreneurial firms. The value of any individual's or firm's capabilities is therefore conditional upon the existence of partners in a network. Firms and workers place a greater value on locations within clusters which contain complementary workers and firms than on those outside of clusters. Such market/locational failure can occur where there is a potential for geographic, inter-sectoral linkages, or networks. One example of this is "YouTube.com" which was created by a University of Illinois graduate who had moved to Silicon Valley.

The second source of market/locational failure involves knowledge externalities. University-generated knowledge is inherently a public good so that its production generates externalities. However, local proximity is essential for accessing these knowledge spillovers.

The third source of market/locational failure associated with entrepreneurship is that positive economic value for third-party firms and individuals is created even when entrepreneurial firms fail. The high failure rate of new-firm start-ups has been widely documented, and the failure rates in knowledge-based activities are especially great.[13]

This is not surprising since knowledge activities are associated with a greater degree of uncertainty. However, the failure of a high technology or knowledge-based firm does not imply that no value was created by that firm. Ideas created by failed firms and projects often become integral parts of successful products and projects in other (successful) firms.

The externalities accruing from failed firms also create a market/locational failure in the valuation of (potential) new enterprises by private investors and policy makers. Whereas the private investor can only appropriate his/her investment if the particular firm succeeds, a failed firm that generates positive externalities contributes to the success of other third-party firms. The private investor, however, does not appropriate anything from the original investment. Likewise, individual firms and workers would have no incentive to invest in the development of a cluster, which is the creation of other entrepreneurial firms, due to their inability to appropriate returns from such a cluster.

From the public policy perspective, on the other hand, it does not matter which firm succeeds, as long as some firms do, and growth, along with the other benefits accruing from entrepreneurship, is generated for that particular region.

The fourth source of market/locational failure involves the demonstration effect emanating from knowledge spillover of entrepreneurial activity. This is particularly valuable in regions where entrepreneurship has been noticeably lacking and where no strong tradition of entrepreneurship exists. Entrepreneurial activity involves not just the firm or the entrepreneurial scientist making the decision to start the firm. Rather, other colleagues will observe the process of opportunity recognition and action in the form of starting a new high-technology firm, along with the results accruing from this entrepreneurial activity. The demonstration externality is in the form of learning by third-party individuals that entrepreneurship is a viable alternative to the status quo. As a result of this demonstration effect, others will be induced to also develop entrepreneurial strategies and perhaps alter their own career trajectories to include an entrepreneurial activity. Thus, there is a strong and compelling positive externality associated with entrepreneurship as a result of the demonstration effect, particularly in regions with no strong entrepreneurial traditions. The demonstration effect focuses primarily on the individual scientist but is also linked to the post-start-up performance of the firm. We would expect the demonstration effect to be greater within a geographically bounded regional context, such as a cluster.

As a result of the market/locational failures inherent in the externalities involved in knowledge spillover entrepreneurship – which stem from networks, knowledge, learning, and demonstration – a gap is created in the valuation of entrepreneurial activities between private parties and the local public policy makers. Just as what has been identified as the existence of liquidity constraints in the form of what they term as "The Valley of Death" and the "Darwinian Sea," it may be that the financing constraints confronting not just the new and young enterprises but also potential entrepreneurs are even more severe in regions outside of a knowledge cluster than for their counterparts located within a knowledge cluster.

The role that knowledge spillover entrepreneurship plays as a conduit of knowledge spillovers, combined with the strong propensity for those knowledge spillovers to be geographically bounded and remain localized, suggests a special focus of public policy on the impact of local institutions, universities, and policies on the cognitive process of changing career trajectories and making a decision to become an entrepreneur. By filling the gaps created by the inherent market/locational failure, public policy can create a virtuous entrepreneurial circle, where entrepreneurs become networked and linked to each other and provide strong role models of knowledge spillover entrepreneurship for the local scientific community to emulate.

State and regional policy can contribute to creating entrepreneurship capital in a number of ways. First, it is essential that investments in the inner two circles of Figure 1 be at sufficiently high levels to generate basic and applied research. Second, effective and creative mechanisms in the third, or outermost circle must be developed to facilitate the spillover and transfer of knowledge for commercialization from the universities to the local and state economies. Third, absorptive capacity mechanisms and institutions outside of the university that will be quick and effective in recognizing valuable new ideas and implementing them commercially must also be developed.

However, an additional key role for policy is to ensure that the boundaries between these different layers of the entrepreneurial university and its external environment are as porous as possible. By cre-

ating linkages, interactions and networks across all of these boundaries, policy can make a vital contribution to creating rich entrepreneurship capital facilitating the spillover of knowledge that generates
growth and employment.

An example of a cross-boundary linkage mechanism is the Indiana
Venture Center, which is a public/private non-profit partnership involving Indiana's five research universities and industry. The explicit
mandate of the Venture Center is to make the state more innovative
and entrepreneurial by leveraging the knowledge assets of the universities and helping them to transform those knowledge assets into state-
based economic growth.

Similarly, the Stanford Technology Ventures Program and Stanford's Bio-design Network attempt to link scientists and researchers in
the inner two circles with venture capitalists, attorneys, and other professionals outside of the universities. Yet another example of a linking
mechanism is provided by the Georgia Research Alliance, which is a
research and technology transfer consortium that includes Georgia's
research universities. It has a number of creative programs that help
create and attract entrepreneurs to the state. Through its Eminent
Scholars program, for example, the Georgia Research Alliance brings
to the state renowned scientists from all over the world to lead programs at universities that have potential for significant economic impact for the state. The alliance also invests in numerous research and
development labs that eventually become the basis for development of
new technologies and businesses. As one of the state's most valuable
entrepreneurship resources, the Alliance has contributed to the creation of more than 3000 technology jobs and 90 technology-based
firms.

Thus, the entrepreneurial university can be leveraged to create state
entrepreneurship capital. Universities are talent magnets. The great
universities have always attracted an amalgam of creative and innovative minds. One of the things that we have learned is that people will
move to places that offer attractive amenities (including parks, moun-
tains, etc.). Transportation infrastructure is also vital to facilitating a
concentration of human capital. But now, with porous boundaries, that
concentration of creativity and knowledge created in the traditional
disciplines at the core of the university can be linked to external applications. Entrepreneurship serves as the conduit for precious invest-

ments in knowledge, ideas, and creativity to spillover for commercial application and ultimately state economic growth.

Conclusions

Something of a new consensus is emerging in Europe that they, too, need an entrepreneurial university system that is compatible with an entrepreneurial Europe. According to the publisher-editor, Josef Joffe, of one of the most important German newspapers, *Die Zeit*, "A hundred years ago Humboldt University in Berlin was the model for the rest of the world. Todyo, Johns Hopkins, Stanford and the University of Chicago were founded in conscious imitation of the German university and its novel fusion of teaching and research. Today Europe's universities have lost their luster, and as they talk reform, they talk American. Indeed, America is one huge global 'demonstration effect,' as the sociologists call it."[14]

In response to this newly emerging consensus that the old university model no longer suffices, Germany introduced a bold new policy to move towards the entrepreneurial university. This new public policy approach is a striking rejection of the post-war policies of homogeneity and standardization, with the concomitant result of curbing competition across institutions. Rather, this new policy approach injects competition across universities through the introduction of a policy instrument called the *Exzellenzinitiative*, or Excellence Initiative. Over a five year period, staring in 2005, the German government is investing 1.9 billion Euros to explicitly create what is termed as Elite Universities. These funds will be awarded to those universities that have developed at least the potential for excellence in research in particular research fields.[15]

After years of perhaps admiring in particular the top American Universities, but writing them off as another example of American elitism and exclusivity, to the disadvantage of those not afforded access to such universities, the Germans have radically reversed directions and are now embracing "elite" universities. The old approach would have been to spread the funding around, in a virtual quota system, where each region got its share. But under this new policy, instead, these new elite universities are concentrated particularly in the state of Bavaria, where several universities, including the Ludwig-Maximilians-University of Munich and the Technical University of Munich were selected along with eight other German universities to be targeted for becoming "elite."

Why has Germany reversed its policy towards higher education and research? Because it recognizes that in the global economy, the old, traditional Humboldt style university, which is cut off from society, does not suffice. Rather, Germany, like countries around the globe is now committed to create the entrepreneurial university. According to the Federal Minister of Education in Germany, Annette Schavan, "The German Government needs to force scientific research and the economy to work together. The goal is to start a common innovation strategy to develop a science-based high-technology strategy."[16]

Germany spent too many years on the sidelines, saddled with a policy approach inhibiting not just state-of-the-art research and scholarship, but also their commercialization and application in the economy. As The Wall Street Journal reports, "Political leaders and economists across the continent say that weak links to business, funding shortages and lack of competition for staff and students at universities are threatening to erode the technological edge the continent needs to compete globally."[17] According to Janez Potocnik, who serves as the European Commissioner for Science and Research concludes from looking across to the other side of the Atlantic, "Our universities must be able to respond to the demands of the market. We have fallen behind."[18] According, in May 2006 the European Commission identified increasing not only the funding of universities and research but also the commercialization of that research as a high priority for Europe. It has turned out that the investment that the United States has made in universities and research was not just an extravagant expenditure but rather the foundation for generating growth and competitiveness in the global economy.

Georg Winckler, President of the European Conference of University Presidents, emphasizes that in this new century, "The higher is the level of education and human capital of citizens, the higher will be the standard of living. Human capital and education are the most important source of a high standard of living. Europe is suffering from a clear deficit of such human capital and education... In contrast to the United States there is too low of a share of the European population with a degree in higher education."[19] Winckler goes on to point out that the Nobel Prize is typically awarded to an American, or rather someone living and working in the United States.

In France, for example, the government allocates around $8,500 annually per university student, which is 40 percent less than the investment made in each high school student.[20] Whether Germany and other European countries can catch up and compensate for too many years of passively watching and shaking their heads of the transformation of American universities and colleges remains to be seen. On the one hand, students complain about the quality of university courses and the inaccessibility to professors and the research process. On the other hand, as *The New York Times* reports of a French university student who was asked about his willingness to pay more tuition in exchange for a better university experience, "The University is a public service. The state must pay."[21]

Still, in 2003 universities in the United Kingdom began charging student fees of pounds 3,000, or $5,685, although exemptions were allowed for financially impoverished students. Similarly, a court decision in Germany in 2005 has paved the way for some universities to start charging tuition, even if it is only 1,000 Euros per year.[22]

But one thing is becoming clear from the recent and startling revolution that is now beginning to shake up the sleepy European universities. The entrepreneurial university has emerged as a central institution and source of not just scientific and knowledge but also cultural and social thinking and values in helping to create the entrepreneurial society.

Public policy is responding to take advantages of the opportunities afforded by globalization rather than being victimized by globalization. In order to generate sustainable growth, employment and competitiveness in a globalized economy, public policy has been refocusing on investments in knowledge, such as education, research, human capital, culture and creativity. The role of the university is changing in two important ways. First, the university has emerged as an important source of knowledge, creativity and ideas that drive economic growth and employment. Second, the university plays a key role in the creation of an entrepreneurial society, which ensures that society will actually realize a return on its investments in creating new knowledge.

Endnotes

[1] Solow, Robert (1956), "A Contribution to Theory of Economic Growth", Quarterly Journal of Economics, 70, 65-94.

[2] Solow, Robert (1957), "Technical Change and the Aggregate Production Function", *Review of Economics and Statistics, 39*, 312-320

[3] Romer, Paul. "Increasing Returns and Long-run Growth." Journal of Political Economy (1994): 1002-1037.

[4] *Lucas, Robert (1993), "Making a Miracle," Econometrica, 61, 251-272.*

[5] Introductory statement of Birch Bayh, September 13, 1978, cited from the Association of University Technology Managers Report (AUTM) (2004, p. 5).

[6] Statement by Birch Bayh, (April 13, 1980), on the approval of S. 414 (Bayh-Dole) by the U.S. Senate on a 91-4 vote, cited from (AUTM) (2004, p. 16).

[7] Audretsch, David B., Max Keilbach and Erik Lehmann (2006), Entrepreneurship and Economic Growth, (New York: Oxford University Press).

[8] Audretsch, David B. (2007a), The Entrepreneurial Society, (New York: Oxford University Press).

[9] See Rothaermel, Frank T., Shanti Dewi Anak Agung Istri, and Lin Jiang. "University Entrepreneurship: Taxonomy of the Literature." Industrial and Corporate Change, 2007.

[10] The Humboldt University of Berlin (German Humboldt-Universität zu Berlin), founded in 1810, is Berlin's oldest university. The structure of Humboldt, with its emphasis on basic research, served as a model for institutions like Harvard, Duke, and Cornell.

[11] The Morril Act provided for, ". . . *the endowment, support, and maintenance of at least one college where the leading object shall be, without excluding other* scientific *and classical studies, and including military tactics, to teach such branches of learning as are related to agriculture and the mechanic arts, in such manner as the legislatures of the states may respectively prescribe, in order to promote the liberal and practical education of the industrial classes in the several pursuits and professions in life.*"

[12] Each state was granted 30,000 acres of public land for each Senator and Representative then in office. Thus the minimum amount of land granted is 90,000 acres: two senators and one representative. Most states received much more land for their new universities.

[13] Caves, Richard. "Industrial Organization and New Findings on the Turnover and Mobility of Firms." *Journal of Economic Literature*, 36 (1998): 1947-82.

[14] Josef Joffee, "The Perils of Soft Power: Why America's Cultural Influence Makes Enemies, Too," *New York Times Magazine*, May 14, 2006, p. 15.

[15] "Der Triumph des Südens", Focus, No. 5, 30 January, 2006, pp. 48-49.

[16] Ministerin Schavan: Dialog Zwischen Wissenschaft und Wirtschaft forcieren, *Deutschland Nachrichten* , May 22, 2006.

[17] John W. Miller, "Europe's Flat Learning Curve: Innovation Wants for Funding, Tighter University-Business Ties," *The Wall Street Journal*, May 16, 2002, pp. A7-A8, p. A7.

[18] Ibid.

[19] "Entscheidend ist die Bereitschaft neues Wissen anzunehmen," *Frankfurter Allgemeine*, March 11, 2006, p. 12.

[20] Elaine Scioloino, "Higher Learning in France Clings to its Old Ways," *The New York Times*, May 12, 2006, p. A1, p. 1, A16.

[21] Ibid.

[22] See EN 17.

8

Globalization and Higher Education: A Regional Perspective

Alan M. Rugman

Today universities in Europe and North America operate in a business environment characterized by globalization. By globalization is meant a high degree of economic interdependence facilitated through increases in international trade and foreign direct investment. Some writers argue that this trend of increasing economic interdependence is leading to greater commonality in social and cultural areas, as well as in economic ones. In fact, most economic activity takes place within each of the broad triad regions of the EU, North America, and the Asia Pacific. Of the world's largest 500 firms there are 380 providing data on the geographic distribution of their sales and assets. Of these, 320 firms average 80% of their sales in their home region. Only nine are global firms in the sense of having at least 20% of their sales in each broad triad region. Therefore, a more sophisticated view of globalization is that the world's leading firms have expanded their trade and foreign direct investment mainly on an intra-regional basis. What are the implications of this for higher education?

The university today is regarded as a vehicle to generate knowledge. In terms of public policy, support for university research is frequently based on the notion that there will be knowledge spillovers. As most university research funding is generated by national government agencies and by home country firms, most assessments of the value of university research and knowledge generation have taken the country as the unit of analysis. Yet the logic of the first paragraph is that the appropriate unit of analysis is the broad region of the triad. This leads to the following types of questions:

(1) Within the EU to what extent has university education and research led to productivity increases in member states?

(2) To what extent has the economic integration of the EU led to an internal market for the graduates of European universities in a manner similar to that of the United States? Are there remaining barriers to the free mobility of labor in higher education in Europe? How long will it be before Germany develops MBA programs to produce managers at the level of the United Kingdom (which already has 100 universities with MBA programs)?

(3) What is the contribution of universities to knowledge creation in the economic clusters which today dominate world business? Is there a Silicon Valley in Europe? To what extent has public policy in the EU been able to bring together business and universities in the development of successful knowledge clusters? Are there examples of clusters in life sciences to match clusters in manufacturing?

(4) To what extent has higher education in Europe matched the focus on entrepreneurship which is a characteristic of North American business? How much focus is there in European universities on the development of entrepreneurship? Or is there still a focus on government support?

(5) In comparisons of the role of higher education between Europe and North America, to what extent is the experience in Asia of relevance? Today, many Asian countries are making huge investments in higher education leading to a large output of highly-qualified engineers, information technology experts and related skills. In addition many Asian universities are now creating business schools in order to train a new generation of managers. Some European and American universities act as partners in these new institutional developments. These are similar to joint ventures and strategic alliances, but what are the long-term cost and benefits of such partnerships? Is the Asian partner able to appropriate the knowledge, brand, and or other attributes of the European and American partner? And If so, how quickly? Are there any mecha-

nisms which can be introduced to safeguard against such potential losses of institutional resources?

Does Globalization Mean the World is Flat?

A large academic literature in the international business field suggests that multinational enterprises (MNEs) are the key drivers of globalization.[1] Yet many popular books on globalization fail to recognize the nature, extent and business reality of MNEs as leaders of globalization.

Perhaps the most influential of these books is that by New York Times journalist, Thomas Friedman, *The World is Flat*[2]. It has been reported that over three million copies have been sold; yet this book is based upon a faulty understanding of globalization. It lacks any insight and balance into the underlying empirical context of world business. Here Friedman's model is summarized and I then develop a new framework to better analyze it.

Basically, Friedman makes one point in his book, namely, today a large proportion of international business takes place through offshoring. There are two main sites for offshoring. First, much manufacturing and cost innovation takes place in China. Second, many service sector activities, especially in information technology sectors, take place in India. While both types of offshoring certainly exist (and are explained by factor cost conditions) it is apparent that Friedman vastly exaggerates the importance of offshoring beyond the information technology related area. His book largely consists of interesting and well-written anecdotes referring to this particular sector.

A Framework for The World is Flat

As can be seen in Table 1a, Friedman develops an argument that today the world is characterized by globalization 3.0. This is a situation where individuals are empowered to run global businesses. They can process information and organize activities with the use of personal computers and the Internet. This type of globalization has replaced globalization 2.0 in which multinational enterprises organized international activity. During this era of globalization 2.0 which lasted from 1800 to 2000, MNEs grew and benefited from falling transportation costs (the development of railroads, bulk shipping lines, jet aircraft) and falling telecommunications. Previous to this type of globalization, according to Friedman, there existed globalization 1.0. This lasted from 1492 to 1800. International exchange was organized across and between countries. International trade was largely explained by labor cost differentials and the existence of natural resources.

Table 1a. Friedman's Flat World Model

Globalization 1.0 1492-1800: Labor costs and natural resources	Country level
Globalization 2.0 1800-2000: Multinational enterprises Falling transportation costs Falling telecommunication costs	Firm level
Globalization 3.0 2000 to date: Personal computers and Internet	Individual level

The theoretical logic behind Friedman's flat world model (to the extent that there is any theory) would be as follows: globalization 1.0 is largely explained by international economics and the principle of comparative advantage. Countries specialized in the export of goods which use intensively their abundant factor (e.g. cheap labor or mineral deposits). Globalization 2.0 is explained by theories of international business (MNEs internalize knowledge advantages and control these firm-specific advantages within wholly-owned subsidiaries). Globalization 3.0 essentially has no theoretical support. It appears to assume that information exchange is free and that there are no barriers to entry in doing business anywhere in the world. Clearly globalization 3.0 presents many challenges, and these are discussed in more detail later in this paper.

In Figure 1, these three types of globalization are synthesized in a new matrix. On the horizontal axis I put the Internet which is available to a low or high degree. On the vertical axis I represent the presence of multinational enterprises, again, to a low or high degree. In cell 2 Friedman globalization 1.0 appears; neither MNEs nor the Internet are important. In cell 1, globalization 2.0 appears. Here the role of MNEs is predominant, while the Internet is unimportant. In cell 4, globalization 3.0 appears. Friedman argues that only the Internet matters and that MNEs have been replaced by individual business activity.

Figure 1: Friedman's Three Types of Globalization

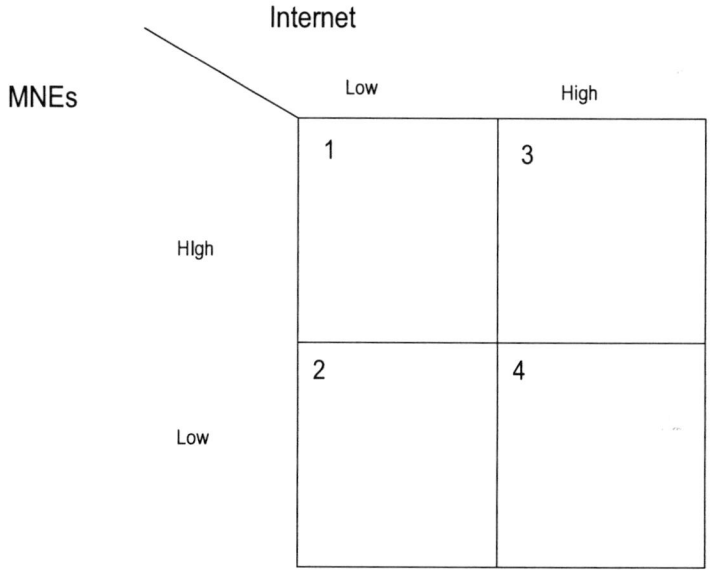

In Friedman's book cell 3 is not discussed; yet, this is clearly the cell where international business activity now takes place. In reality, individuals lack the financial resources, institutional learning advantages, and managerial expertise to build global businesses. Instead, in cell 3 both MNEs and the Internet are important. MNEs are better equipped than individuals to overcome the remaining frictions which constrain world business. These are in the form of government regulations, cultural and religious differences, and the persistence of historical and nationalist tendencies. While the Internet provides information on these issues it does not provide a mechanism to overcome them. In contrast, the MNE is better equipped to analyze and respond to such persistent differences. As shown below the business world is largely divided into three broad regions of the triad. Doing business between the triad regions is extremely difficult. Only MNEs are able to tackle these triad barriers.

Figure 2: The FSA/CSA Matrix

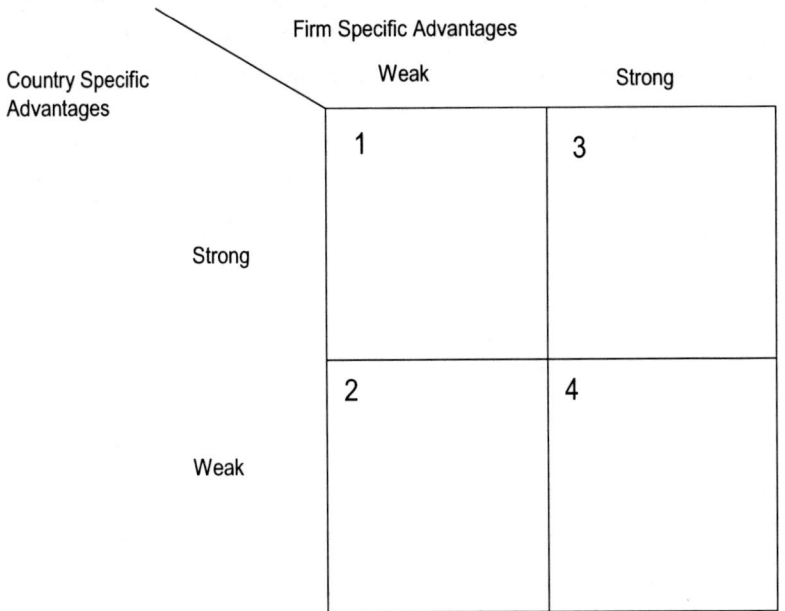

Source: A.M. Rugman and S.C. Collinson, International Business (4th ed.) London: Pearson pp. 49-52, based on A.M. Rugman, Inside the Multinationals. New York: Columbia University Press, 1981.

Building on this analysis, it is useful to reinterpret Friedman within the basic model used in the field of international business. This is the matrix relating country to firm factors, as first developed by Rugman.[3] This is reported in Figure 2 where country-specific advantages (CSAs) are shown on the vertical axis and firm-specific advantages (FSAs) on the horizontal axis. It is incorrect to generalize the country effect (the CSA axis in my Figure 2) and make it the sole explanation of globalization. Instead, the firm effects need to be brought together, as in cell

3 of Figure 3. It can be seen that Friedman's book is mainly about cell 1, and that he presents no evidence of the way FSAs can be developed such that CSAs in China and India are transformed by emerging economy MNEs into cell 3 firm-specific attributes.

This analysis counters the simplistic notions of writers such as Thomas Friedman. The world is not flat. International business suggests that there remain strong barriers as a business attempts to cross the boundaries of triad regions. It is pointless to assume globalization; instead, it is necessary to investigate the manner in which a firm's business model may need to be adapted such that its FSAs can overcome the liability of inter-regional foreignness.

The Lexus and the Olive Tree

In an earlier influential book by Thomas Friedman, *The Lexus and the Olive Tree*[4], he uses the Lexus as a symbol for economic integration. In contrast, the olive tree is a symbol for the historical, political, religious and social aspects which present obstacles to economic integration. Therefore, the logic of the Lexus view of globalization would fit on the vertical axis of Figure 3, whereas the olive tree would be assigned to the horizontal axis representing a need for national responsiveness. Friedman himself discusses the extreme cases of the Lexus in cell 1 and the olive tree in cell 4. However, based on our analysis of Figure 3 it is apparent that cell 3 represents another interesting case where both globalization and national responsiveness are equally important. The other point is that Figure 3 is a strategy diagram to be put into operation by managers of MNEs (or other firms). Therefore, it is the interpretation of the Lexus and the olive tree axes which is important for strategic management. A potential for strategy in cell 3 would require that an MNE is able to organize itself to cope with both axes.

In his later work Friedman argues that the olive tree is no longer relevant and that only globalization matters. In his book, The World is Flat, Friedman is only interested in outsourcing and globalization, where the latter is driven by the Internet and individual use of personal computers such that business can be done globally. By reverting to analysis of only the vertical axis of Figures 2 and 3, Friedman has ignored the complexities of globalization and vastly exaggerated the flat nature of the world's economy. Data confirm the fact that the world is regional, not global.[5]

Figure 3: Globalization and Nationalism

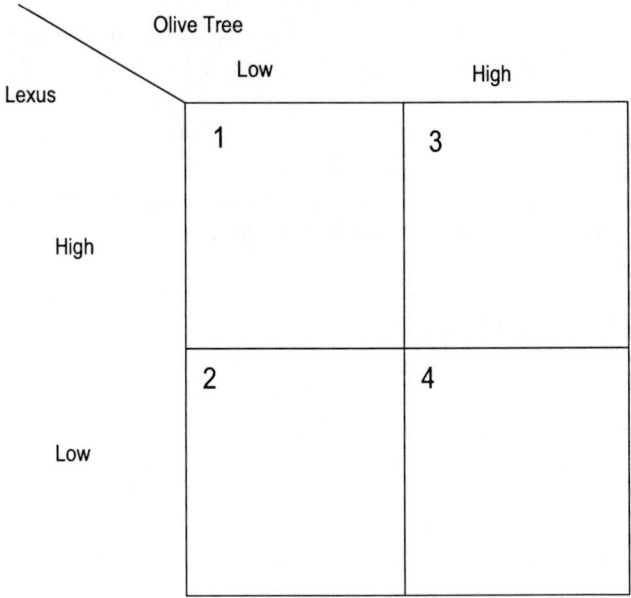

The Empirical Evidence on Regionalization

Table 1b reports the geographic sales of the world's 500 largest MNEs, based on the data bank.[6] Briefly, in this databank there is information on the geographic sales of 380 of the world's 500 largest firms. Of these 380 firms, 335 provide information on their sales in North America. Of these firms, 185 are North American MNEs (mostly from the United States with 15 from Canada and 1 from Mexico). These 185 firms average 72 % of their sales in North America; 14 % in Europe; and 6 % in Asia Pacific. In contrast, the 150 European and Asian MNEs average 21 % of their sales in North America. Of these, 99 European MNEs average 64 % of their sales in Europe. The 51 Asian MNEs average 73 % of their sales in Asia Pacific.

Table 1b: Sales of Multinational Enterprises in North America

Company Name	Number of MNEs	Revenue in bn US$	North America % of total	Europe % of total	Asia-Pacific % of total
Total 500 MNEs	335	30.7	52.4	32.1	23.0
North American MNEs	185	28.8	**78.1**	13.9	5.6
European and Asian MNEs	150	33.1	20.8	46.4	36.2
European	99	33.0	22.8	**63.6**	7.9
Asian	51	33.3	16.9	7.8	**73.0**

Source: Authors' calculation based on Rugman (2005*) The Regional Multinationals: MNEs and Global Strategic Management*.
Note. The values are calculated only when an MNE reports its regional sales in North America.
Data are for 2001

The average size of the two sets of firms is approximately the same. The 185 North American MNEs average $29 billion in sales, whereas the 150 foreign MNEs average $33 billion in sales. We will now analyze the sales of these firms in more detail. There are 47 North American firms with 100 % of their sales in North America (i.e. they are purely home triad region based). These include: retail firms like Home Depot, Kroger, Sears Roebuck, Target, Kmart, and Safeway; financials like State Farm, Allstate, Aetna, Bank One, Wachovia, U.S. Bancorp; and energy firms like Sunoco, Power Corp, Allegheny Energy, etc. These firms average $21.7 billion of sales in North America. There are 27 North American firms with between 90 to 99.9 % of their sales in North America, averaging $37 billion of sales in North America. Then there are 23 firms with between 80 and 89.9 % of their sales in North America, etc.

Over half (97) of the set of 185 North American firms have over 80 % of their sales in North America. Only one European (Delhaize 'Le Lion') and one Australian firm (News Corp) can match their focus on North America. Indeed, 49 European firms and 35 Asian firms have less than 20 % of their sales in North America, which is too low a percentage to be of much strategic significance to these firms. However, a total of 50 European and 16 other firms have more than a 20 %

presence in North America. These 66 firms are the firms which are the key rivals of North American firms in the North America region. The ten non-North American firms with over 50 % of their sales (shown in parentheses) in North America are:

Delhaize 'Le Lion'	*Europe*	*75.9*
News Corp.	Asia-Pacific	75.0
Wolseley	Europe	66.3
DaimlerChrysler	Europe	60.1
Royal Ahold	Europe	59.2
Santander Central Hispano Group	Europe	55.7
Honda Motor	Asia-Pacific	53.9
AstraZeneca	Europe	52.8
ING Group	Europe	51.4
Sodexho Alliance	Europe	50.0

In Table 2 below there is further analysis of the sales of 150 foreign MNEs active in North America. Six of these firms have total sales of over $100 billion. Of these DaimlerChrysler has total sales of $137 billion of which 60 % are in North America; BP has worldwide sales of $174 billion of which $48 billion are in North America; Toyota has sales of $121 billion of which 36.6 % are in North America; Shell has sales of $135 billion of which 15.6 % are in North America. In contrast, the two giant Japanese firms, Mitsui and Mitsubishi, only have 7 % and 4 % respectively in North America. Overall, the average sales of these 150 foreign MNEs in North America is 22.46 %.

Table 2: Regional Sales of 150 Foreign MNEs in North America

Company Name	Region	Revenue in bn US$	North America % of total	Europe % of total	Asia-Pacific % of total
BP	Europe	174.2	48.1	36.3	na
DaimlerChrysler	Europe	136.9	60.1	29.9	na
Royal Dutch/Shell Group	Europe	135.2	15.6	46.1	na
Toyota Motor	Asia-Pacific	120.8	36.6	7.7	49.2
Mitsubishi	Asia-Pacific	105.8	5.4	1.7	86.8
Mitsui	Asia-Pacific	101.2	7.4	11.1	78.9
Total Fina Elf	Europe	94.3	8.4	55.6	na
Itochu	Asia-Pacific	91.2	5.5	1.7	91.2
Allianz	Europe	85.9	17.6	78.0	4.4
ING Group	Europe	83.0	51.4	35.1	3.4
Volkswagen	Europe	79.3	20.1	68.2	5.3
Siemens	Europe	77.4	30.0	52.0	13.0
Sumitomo	Asia-Pacific	77.1	4.8	na	87.3
Marubeni	Asia-Pacific	71.8	11.6	na	74.5
Deutsche Bank	Europe	66.8	29.3	63.1	6.5
E.ON	Europe	66.5	9.4	80.1	na
AXA	Europe	65.6	24.1	51.2	19.9
Credit Suisse	Europe	64.2	34.9	60.9	4.1
Hitachi	Asia-Pacific	63.9	11.0	7.0	80.0
Sony	Asia-Pacific	60.6	29.8	20.2	32.8
Royal Ahold	Europe	59.6	59.2	32.8	0.6
Honda Motor	Asia-Pacific	58.9	53.9	8.1	26.9
Matsushita	Asia-	55.0	12.4	6.9	64.9

Company Name	Region	Revenue in bn US$	North America % of total	Europe % of total	Asia-Pacific % of total
Electric Industrial	Pacific				
Fiat	Europe	51.9	13.0	73.3	na
Vivendi Universal	Europe	51.4	22.0	68.0	na
Assicurazioni Generali	Europe	51.4	1.7	91.4	na
RWE	Europe	50.7	19.5	75.0	5.1
Nestlé	Europe	50.2	31.4	31.6	na
Nissan Motor	Asia-Pacific	49.6	34.6	11.0	49.7
UBS	Europe	48.5	37.0	58.0	5.0
Unilever	Europe	46.1	46.6	38.7	15.4
ENI	Europe	44.6	12.1	80.4	3.1
Metro	Europe	44.3	-	97.3	2.3
Nissho Iwai	Asia-Pacific	43.7	7.5	3.0	88.9
Deutsche Telekom	Europe	43.2	6.3	93.1	na
Toshiba	Asia-Pacific	43.1	13.9	8.7	75.3
Munich Re Group	Europe	41.9	19.3	72.3	4.1
Mizuho Holdings	Asia-Pacific	41.5	19.7	5.8	74.4
NEC	Asia-Pacific	40.8	7.0	na	79.6
Fortis	Europe	40.5	21.4	64.3	na
Fujitsu	Asia-Pacific	40.0	11.4	12.2	71.8
Zurich Financial Services	Europe	38.7	38.3	51.0	na
Suez	Europe	37.9	11.0	74.0	5.0
BMW	Europe	34.4	31.7	57.3	na
Tesco	Europe	33.9	-	93.6	6.4
Royal Bank of Scotland	Europe	33.8	12.0	81.0	na

Company Name	Region	Revenue in bn US$	North America % of total	Europe % of total	Asia-Pacific % of total
Thyssen Krupp	Europe	33.8	21.9	61.1	na
Vodafone	Europe	32.7	0.1	93.1	4.8
Deutsche Post	Europe	31.3	5.0	91.6	2.7
Hyundai Motor	Asia-Pacific	30.9	18.1	0.3	81.6
Santander Central Hispano Group	Europe	30.4	55.7	44.3	na
Sumitomo Mitsui Banking	Asia-Pacific	30.2	11.1	5.6	83.4
BT	Europe	30.0	8.3	87.0	4.7
GlaxoSmith-Kline	Europe	29.5	49.2	28.6	na
Mitsubishi Electric	Asia-Pacific	29.2	8.9	6.0	83.1
BASF	Europe	29.1	23.6	55.3	14.4
Royal Philips Electronics	Europe	29.0	28.7	43.0	21.5
Nokia	Europe	27.9	25.0	49.0	26.0
Telefónica	Europe	27.8	-	56.9	-
EADS	Europe	27.6	33.7	44.9	10.2
Barclays	Europe	27.6	6.0	88.0	na
Saint-Gobain	Europe	27.2	22.3	63.9	na
Bayer	Europe	27.1	32.7	40.3	16.1
Ito-Yokado	Asia-Pacific	26.8	30.2	na	66.6
Statoil	Europe	26.3	10.0	86.8	na
Mitsubishi Tokyo Financial Group	Asia-Pacific	26.1	23.6	7.0	64.4
Enel	Europe	25.8	0.2	98.6	na
Mitsubishi Motors	Asia-Pacific	25.6	22.1	12.1	62.8
UFJ Holdings	Asia-Pacific	25.3	15.5	6.1	78.5
Groupe Pinault-Printemps	Europe	24.9	21.2	69.1	5.6

Company Name	Region	Revenue in bn US$	North America % of total	Europe % of total	Asia-Pacific % of total
J. Sainsbury	Europe	24.6	16.7	83.3	-
Canon	Asia-Pacific	23.9	33.8	20.8	28.5
Société Générale	Europe	23.9	15.6	77.3	3.6
Commerzbank	Europe	23.8	8.5	85.5	3.0
ABB	Europe	23.7	25.1	53.9	11.3
Nippon Mitsubishi Oil	Asia-Pacific	23.5	1.9	10.2	87.9
Westdeutsche Landesbank	Europe	23.1	12.8	80.0	5.1
Mitsubishi Heavy Industries	Asia-Pacific	22.9	4.7	1.9	93.2
Alcatel	Europe	22.7	19.8	62.9	7.4
L.M. Ericsson	Europe	22.4	13.2	46.0	25.9
Hyundai	Asia-Pacific	21.7	24.2	10.5	56.3
Royal & Sun Alliance	Europe	21.5	27.1	64.8	na
Alstom	Europe	20.7	28.0	45.1	16.1
Aventis	Europe	20.5	38.8	32.1	6.4
East Japan Railway	Asia-Pacific	20.3	-	-	100.0
Daiei	Asia-Pacific	20.1	0.5	-	99.5
Delhaize 'Le Lion'	Europe	19.6	75.9	22.0	1.0
Denso	Asia-Pacific	19.2	20.0	6.8	73.1
Novartis	Europe	19.0	43.0	32.0	na
Crédit Lyonnais	Europe	18.8	8.0	82.0	7.0
Diageo	Europe	18.6	49.9	31.8	7.7
Bouygues	Europe	18.3	2.0	62.0	13.0
Volvo	Europe	18.3	30.2	51.6	6.0
Centrica	Europe	18.2	6.2	93.8	na
Almanij	Europe	18.1	1.9	97.9	-

Company Name	Region	Revenue in bn US$	North America % of total	Europe % of total	Asia-Pacific % of total
Bertelsmann	Europe	17.9	32.2	62.1	na
Abbey National	Europe	17.8	0.5	99.5	-
BHP Billiton	Asia-Pacific	17.8	12.6	13.0	66.1
Bridgestone	Asia-Pacific	17.6	43.0	10.1	38.8
Roche Group	Europe	17.3	38.6	36.8	11.7
Norsk Hydro	Europe	17.0	11.8	77.0	4.2
Sanyo Electric	Asia-Pacific	16.9	17.0	8.7	72.7
Landesbank Baden-Wurttemberg	Europe	16.9	2.7	94.8	2.5
Mazda Motor	Asia-Pacific	16.8	24.4	7.0	65.7
AstraZeneca	Europe	16.5	52.8	32.0	5.2
Kajima	Asia-Pacific	16.5	6.9	1.0	92.2
Nichimen	Asia-Pacific	16.4	0.6	2.3	91.5
Vinci	Europe	16.3	5.0	89.0	na
Adecco	Europe	16.1	28.0	60.0	9.0
Kingfisher	Europe	16.1	0.8	98.3	0.6
Skanska	Europe	15.9	41.0	40.0	na
Bayerische Lan-desbank	Europe	15.8	12.9	82.1	5.2
Lufthansa Group	Europe	14.9	19.5	61.7	11.6
Anglo Ameri-can	Europe	14.8	18.9	46.1	17.8
Michelin	Europe	14.6	40.0	47.0	Na
Man Group	Europe	14.6	15.6	68.7	12.7
Sharp	Asia-Pacific	14.4	18.7	9.5	80.0
KarstadtQuelle	Europe	14.4	-	100.0	-
News Corp.	Asia-Pacific	13.8	75.0	16.0	9.0

Company Name	Region	Revenue in bn US$	North America % of total	Europe % of total	Asia-Pacific % of total
Tohoku Electric Power	Asia-Pacific	13.6	-	-	100.0
Ricoh	Asia-Pacific	13.4	16.4	16.1	60.5
Suzuki Motor	Asia-Pacific	13.3	13.3	14.9	68.4
Electrolux	Europe	13.1	39.0	47.0	9.0
Flextronics International	Asia-Pacific	13.1	46.3	30.9	22.4
BAE Systems	Europe	13.0	32.3	38.1	2.7
Arcelor	Europe	13.0	12.0	75.0	na
Norinchukin Bank	Asia-Pacific	12.9	2.2	7.2	90.6
Isuzu Motors	Asia-Pacific	12.8	39.6	na	69.2
Compass Group	Europe	12.6	32.4	67.6	-
L'Oréal	Europe	12.3	32.4	48.5	na
Lafarge	Europe	12.3	32.0	40.0	8.0
Stora Enso	Europe	12.1	19.5	69.2	7.1
British Airways	Europe	11.9	18.6	64.8	na
Lagardère Groupe	Europe	11.9	20.4	71.1	8.5
Sumitomo Electric Industries	Asia-Pacific	11.9	13.5	na	82.8
Henkel	Europe	11.7	14.8	72.1	8.0
Kyushu Electric Power	Asia-Pacific	11.7	-	-	100.0
Cathay Life	Asia-Pacific	11.6	-	-	100.0
Woolworths	Asia-Pacific	11.5	-	-	100.0
Yasuda Fire & Marine Insurance	Asia-Pacific	11.3	-	-	100.0
Dior (Christian)	Europe	11.3	26.0	36.0	32.0
Corus Group	Europe	11.1	11.5	82.7	5.8

Company Name	Region	Revenue in bn US$	North America % of total	Europe % of total	Asia-Pacific % of total
LVMH	Europe	11.0	26.0	36.0	32.0
Danske Bank Group	Europe	10.9	5.1	94.3	0.6
Fuji Heavy Industries	Asia-Pacific	10.9	33.7	na	66.0
Norddeutsche Landesb.	Europe	10.6	2.9	94.8	2.3
Sodexho Alliance	Europe	10.6	50.0	42.0	na
Alliance Unichem	Europe	10.5	-	100.0	-
Wolseley	Europe	10.4	66.3	28.7	na
Asahi Glass	Asia-Pacific	10.1	12.1	13.4	74.5

Source: Rugman (2005) The Regional Multinationals: MNEs and Global Strategic Management.
Note. The table excludes 130 European and Asian MNEs that do not report their geographic sales in North America. Data are for 2001.

Table 3 further decomposes Table 2. Although Delhaize 'Le Lion' is the non North American firm with the highest percentage of its sales in North America (at 75.9 %), its actual sales are $15 billion in North America, out of its total sales of $20 billion. But there are 17 foreign MNEs with even higher sales in North America topped by BP. We can find (in the last column of Table 3) that the sales presence of BP in North America is $83.8 billion; DaimlerChrysler in North America is $82.3 billion; Toyota is $44.2 billion; ING Group is $42.7 billion; Honda is $31.7 billion; Credit Suisse is 22.4 billion, etc. In Table 3 there are 23 foreign firms identified, each with over ten billions of sales in the year 2001. Data for the other foreign firms, with sales over two billion but below ten billion in North America are not reported.

Table 3: The Sales of Large Foreign Firms in North America

Company Name	Country	North America % of total	Sales in N.A. in bn US$
BP	Britain	48.1	83.8
DaimlerChrysler	Germany	60.1	82.3
Toyota Motor	Japan	36.6	44.2
ING Group	Netherland	51.4	42.7
Royal Ahold	Netherland	59.2	35.3
Honda Motor	Japan	53.9	31.7
Siemens	Germany	30.0	23.2
Credit Suisse	Switzerland	34.9	22.4
Unilever	Britain-Netherland	46.6	21.5
Deutsche Bank	Germany	29.3	19.6
Sony	Japan	29.8	18.1
UBS	Switzerland	37.0	17.9
Nissan Motor	Japan	34.6	17.1
Santander Central Hispano Group	Spain	55.7	16.9
Volkswagen	Germany	20.1	15.9
AXA	France	24.1	15.8
Nestlé	Switzerland	31.4	15.8
Delhaize 'Le Lion'	Belgium	75.9	14.9
Zurich Financial Services	Switzerland	38.3	14.8
GlaxoSmithKline	Britain	49.2	14.5
Vivendi Universal	France	22.0	11.3
BMW	Germany	31.7	10.9
News Corp.	Australia	75.0	10.3

Source: Rugman (2005) The Regional Multinationals: MNEs and Global Strategic Management. Data are for 2001.
Note: Ranking is by sales in N.A. as measured by revenues.

Table 4 shows that four industry groups in North America now have more foreign-owned MNEs than "home" firms. These are computers; construction; motor vehicles; banks. Another sector, chemicals and pharmaceuticals, shows an even split of foreign and North American firms.

Table 4: Multinationals in North America by Industry Group

Industry	North America	Europe	Asia-Pacific	Total
Manufacturing Industry				
Aerospace and Defense	12	4	0	16
Chemical and Pharmaceuticals	9	9	0	18
Computer, Office and Electronics	13	6	12	31
Construction and Natural Resources	3	10	2	15
Energy, Petroleum and Refining	20	7	2	29
Food, Drug and Tobacco	12	6	1	19
Motor Vehicle and Parts	10	7	11	28
Other Manufacturing	10	5	2	17
Service Industry				
Banks	11	17	5	33
Merchandisers	31	8	2	41
Other Financial Services	18	7	2	27
Telecommunication and Utilities	12	7	2	21
Other Services	24	6	10	40
Total	185	99	51	335

Source: Authors' calculation based on Rugman (2005) The Regional Multinationals: MNEs and Global Strategic Management.
Note: The values are calculated only when an MNE reports its regional sales in North America. Data are for 2001.

Regionalization and Globalization over Time

The above data are for MNEs for one year, 2001. I have been able to update these data for the world's largest 500 MNEs for the time period, 2001-2004. These data are summarized below. In this section I provide new data across two dimensions. First, I update the sales data from 2001, up to and including 2004. This now provides data for a four-year period for a large number of the world's largest 500 firms. It helps us answer the question about whether there is a trend toward globalization or regionalization. Second, I provide data on assets as well as sales. This is done in order to provide clues about the nature of the upstream (backend) activities of these firms. Some theories suggest that there may be a possible global supply chain and the asset data should therefore provide some more details about this aspect of globalization than the sales (downstream) data previously reported.[7,8] Yet, as will be seen the addition of information on assets provides essentially the same conclusion as for sales: most large firms are home-region based.

In Table 5 for each year I break the data into two categories: manufacturing and services. The number of firms remaining in the population over the four-year period varies by year. The population of firms in the top 500 in year 2001 is reduced from the 380 presented in Rugman (2005) as the set of 500 firms is benchmarked at 2003.[9] Due to mergers and acquisitions, entry and exits according to changes in total revenues there are fewer firms before and after 2003. In Table 5 (Panel A) there are 290 firms but 328 in 2002, 337 in 2003, and 313 in 2004. These numbers reflect the numbers reporting geographic segment information on sales across all four years. In Table 5 (Panel B) there are fewer firms providing data on their geographic segments for assets.

In Table 5 (Panel A) it is shown that the average intra-regional sales figure for all firms is 71.5 % with a plus or minus variation by year of only 0.1 %. There is no significant difference over time, and hence no evidence of a trend towards the globalization of international business activity. However, services average 78.5 % home-region sales as against 63.9 % for manufacturing. This is a statistically significant difference. In Panel B of Table 5 there is, again, no trend towards globalization, but there is a similar statistically significant difference in the average intra-regional assets of services and manufacturing. A two-sample *t-test* shows that the mean values of intra-regional sales for manufacturing (63.9 %) and service industries (78.5 %) over the 2001-2004 period are significantly different at a significance level 1 % for each year. Likewise, the mean values are significantly different for assets.

Table 5: Intra-Regional Sales and Assets of the 500 Firms Over Time

Panel A. Intra-regional Sales

Year	Number of firms	Intra-regional Sales (%)		
		All industries	Manufacturing	Services
2001	290	71.6	64.7	78.5
2002	328	71.4	63.9	78.3
2003	337	71.5	63.2	78.9
2004	313	71.6	63.9	78.4
Weighted Average		71.5	63.9	78.5

Panel B. Intra-regional Assets

Year	Number of firms	Intra-regional Assets (%)		
		All industries	Manufacturing	Services
2001	238	73.4	68.7	78.8
2002	271	73.9	69.4	79.0
2003	282	74.3	69.6	79.3
2004	268	73.7	69.6	78.1
Weighted Average		73.8	69.3	78.8

Source: Annual reports for 2001 – 2004.

The interpretation from both panels of Table 5 is that services are even more home-region oriented than manufacturing across both downstream (sales) and upstream (assets) activities. These data are for the world's largest 500 firms, but, as shown earlier, there is no reason to believe that the large North American MNEs differ in any respect from these findings. All the evidence is that MNEs, in both services and in manufacturing remain based in their home regions. There is no evidence to support a trend towards globalization, in either the upstream (production end) or downstream (customer end) of MNE activity in North America.

Conclusions

In higher education there is a danger that Friedman's simplistic view of globalization will drive University policy. Administrators can become very excited by a flat world and its implications for harmonization of educational practices and policies. Instead, educators need to remember the lasting relevance of Olive Tree thinking. Higher education will need to recognize (and respect) country, and regional differences. Overall, the complexities of the real world, where both global integration and regionalism exist, require educators with agile minds able to think across two dimensions rather than one.

In this paper evidence has been presented to demonstrate that globalization as popularly understood does not exist. There is no evidence that U.S. firms operate globally. Instead, they both produce and sell on a regional basis, as do MNEs from Europe and Asia. There are also present in North America a large set of foreign-owned MNEs that contribute to economic output, but compete with the "home" U.S. MNEs. North America is a battlefield for the world's corporate giants, but with a strong intra-regional effect. The strength of the regional effect is such that analysis of international business strategy needs to distinguish between regional strategy and global strategy. From a North American perspective all Canadian multinationals operate regionally: they need to access the U.S. market in order to be competitive. Even large U.S. firms are found to average some 80 % of their sales in North America. This suggests that NAFTA matters to U.S. firms as well as to Canadian and Mexican ones.

The North American business world is not global, and it is important to contrast NAFTA with the deep economic integration of the EU. While it is highly unlikely that the three members of NAFTA are willing to surrender national sovereignty to the extent achieved by the 27 member states of the EU, it would be useful to have a renewed diplomatic effort to deepen the economic aspects of NAFTA. Such a brief agenda would include the abolition of antidumping and countervailing duty trade remedy laws: inclusion of the agricultural sector in trade liberalization measures: and a new regime to deal with immigration issues. In many ways the economic integration of North America has been led by the business sector. It would now make sense to improve the rules for doing business in North America. NAFTA is now over ten years old, and it is now imperative to reexamine its operation and to improve its institutional fabric.

Endnotes

[1] Rugman, Alan M. (2000). *The End of Globalization*. London: Random House.

[2] Friedman, Thomas L. (2005). *The World is Flat*. New York: Farrar, Straus & Giroux.

[3] Rugman, Alan M. (1981). *Inside the Multinationals: The Economics of Internal Markets*. London: Croom Helm and New York: Columbia University Press.

[4] Friedman, Thomas L. (1999). *The Lexus and the Olive Tree*. New York: Farrar, Straus & Giroux.

[5] *See* Rugman, Alan M. (2005). *The Regional Multinationals*. Cambridge: Cambridge University Press.

[6] Ibid.

[7] Ibid

[8] Rugman, Alan M. and Verbeke, Alan. (2004). "A Perspective on Regional and Global Strategies of Multinational Enterprises", Journal of International Business Studies 35, no. 1, 5-7.

[9] see EN 5

The Changing Nature of Universities: Governance, Competitiveness and Impact

9

University Governance Reform: Academic Policy, Autonomy and Government Regulation

Michael Kelly

Introduction

The term "Governance" can induce a range of emotional responses from glazed eyes through slight interest, passive compliance and enthusiasm! What has it got to do with the agenda around adjusting to globalization currently under discussion?

It may be useful to start with some general principles. Good governance comprising the framework of direction/mission, control, performance management and accountability through which organisations govern their affairs is now seen as an essential part of the management of any enterprise – public, private or not for profit. Because it is principally concerned with setting and maintaining direction and with the management of risk to an enterprise's ability to achieve its goals, it is clearly relevant to the ability of higher education institutions to adapt to changes in their operating environment – which we now regard as global and subject to rapid on-going change.

The last decade has seen a huge shift in attitude on both sides of the Atlantic in relation to the constructive role of strong corporate governance and a significant strengthening of the regulatory environment facing commercial enterprise. Public bodies have also come under the microscope and, while not falling under the shadow of the spectacular failures we have seen in the private world e.g. the Enron/Maxwell's/WorldCom/Parmalat scale disasters, a by-product of those failures is that we are expected to live up to the same principles and standards of governance as are now demanded of listed companies.

Governance Reform and Globalization

The agenda around the challenges of globalization for higher education institutions of course, brings its own new demands. As the international pressure to compete and perform grows stronger, there is an increasing impetus to reform through innovation and in doing so, to move closer to the conventional business model based on a value proposition to the market and away from the more collegiate and reflective approach of the past. This transition puts a new premium on internal quality management and external accreditation processes alongside the need for the normal range of business competencies in the university setting. Maintaining academic credibility, given the multi-faceted nature of the university enterprise, brings particular requirements which do not arise in the conventional corporate business model.

The discernible move internationally from state dominance of funding of Higher Education Institutions (HEIs) to multiple-stream funding, e.g. through income from tuition fees and contracted research, also implies a wider group of interests with a stake in higher education. It is something of an irony that as the public share of overall funding is tending to reduce, the common perception is that the degree of public accountability is tending to increase. That apart, meeting the needs of the growing pool of stakeholders requires stronger and more visible governance structures, within which the distinct but related tasks of pursuing an institution's long-term academic and business goals are made clear.

In looking at HEIs in the context of governance, they bring their own special challenges and demand a customised approach which genuinely reflects a respect for strong autonomous institutions, leaving academic values and decision making to those best qualified to handle them – academics. We need to consider corporate governance and academic governance as linked strands of the overall governance of a university.

Balancing Academic and Business Goals

The combination of the new pressures to perform more robustly in a business sense and the on-going need to preserve academic values can bring some tensions. If a reasonable balance is maintained, this can generate constructive energy for continuous improvement in performance and reputation. If the balance is mismanaged – by an overly ambitious business agenda, an over-bearing president or an overly-conservative academic staff, the prognosis is not as positive, putting it mildly. In my own experience, I have seen both situations at work and would like to share a few observations, based on that experience. To seasoned observers, these may seem like stating the obvious. I mention them as the under-pinning to my own understanding of governance requirements in this new context.

The first is that the corporate model on its own is unlikely to bring about the constructive harmony which yields a progressive campus focussed on quality teaching and academic excellence, combined with a strong business performance ethic. It can provide part of, but not the whole solution.

The second is that strong leaders as well as managers need to be embodied in the gifted people selected as university presidents. Their ability to command respect and to articulate and gain commitment from stakeholders and academic staff to a new vision and mission, to take courageous decisions and to bring people with them, is as important as their financial and organisational skills.

Thirdly, there need to be transparent mechanisms in place which can reconcile managerial and academic goals and resolve any conflicts between them. The respective roles of President, Academic Council (or equivalent) and Governing Board need to be made clear and effective processes put in place to link them.

Fourthly, a competent board with a good understanding of its corporate governance role in providing

- overall strategic direction – in academic and business terms
- overall management oversight
- assurance on risk management and controls; and
- accountability to stakeholders

is a must.

The Board Chair, the Chair of the Academic Council and the President occupy three mutually supportive corners of a triangle. The business of the university cannot succeed without an active and constructive engagement by each.

Ireland

In the Irish system we are currently moving through a transition from a collegiate model to what has been termed by some as "managerialist". This has entailed internal re-structuring; creation typically of a smaller number of schools in place of a larger number of departments within a university and the development of a stronger corporate team supporting the President's role. This has given rise to some tensions – some better managed than others – but I see this process as an essential stage in positioning our universities to use to best effect the public resources made available to them. A particular characteristic of the Irish system, is the continuing dominance of public funding and, as a corollary, a relatively assertive policy role on the part of the state in the affairs of higher education institutions.

As a funder, we expect the universities to play to their respective strengths. We expect them to act strategically but in a way which takes account of public policy goals, alongside institutional ambitions and they are also in their own right required to be fully accountable for their use of public funds.

Our funding dialogue with each college takes place in the context of addressing their strategic aims, including their progress in relation to public goals. We also put a number of dedicated funding streams in place to support particular goals, like access, research development, and strategic innovation. This of itself might be seen as a way of manipulating the strategic intent of a truly autonomous institution, but it might alternatively be seen as a reasonable mechanism for ensuring that public policy goals which underpin public funding streams are explicitly addressed in institutional strategies.

Europe

The whole dialogue at European level on the development of the European Higher Education Area (EHEA) is also built on the principles of respect for strong autonomous institutions enjoying academic freedom and performing a range of roles on behalf of the societies they serve. The new approaches to award recognition, the adoption of the Bologna 3-2-3 cycle, credit transfer and quality assurance processes might be seen as reflecting some further erosion of true institutional autonomy. Again however, the adoption of these harmonising mechanisms in an EHEA is a further reflection of the critical importance now attached particularly to education and research in determining the future of Europe and the imperative for using the combined resources of Europe to best effect in pursing the goals of competitiveness and innovation set out in the Lisbon Agenda.

Conclusion

The stresses and strains of the transition from a collegiate to a more business-like model may ease if we begin to think about good governance as not just something which is virtuous in itself but also brings with it a clarity and a discipline which makes it more likely that we will in fact achieve the goals we set ourselves. This enhancement of capacity in universities to govern their own affairs should also stand to them in responding to the on-going challenges of globalization.

10

Organizational Cultures in U.S. Research-Oriented Universities

Jeffrey A. Hart

Introduction

The governance of any type of organization, including research-oriented universities, is constrained by pre-existing organizational cultures. An organizational culture consists of attitudes, experiences, beliefs, and values shared by members of an organization that are reinforced over time through a variety of practices. Organizational cultures are maintained or altered consciously by leaders, but many are also transmitted from generation to generation without the direct intervention of management.[1]

Two such cultures that strongly affect the governance of universities in the United States are those created by federal funding for research, which I will refer to below as the Vannevar Bush approach (VB for short), and the liberal arts tradition.

The Vannevar Bush Approach and Federal Funding

Vannevar Bush was a prominent intellectual and policy maker during World War II and the early years of the Cold War. He designed and became the first head of the National Defense Research Committee (NDRC) in 1940. The NDRC was absorbed into the Office of Scientific Research and Development (OSRD) in 1941, which Bush also headed. One of the responsibilities of the OSRD was to oversee the Manhattan Project. The OSRD shrank in size and importance after the end of World War II. Bush moved on to become head of the Carnegie Institution of Washington. In 1947, President Truman vetoed a bill, supported by Bush, proposing the conversion of the OSRD into a National Science Foundation (NSF), because he thought the proposed NSF was not sufficiently accountable to the executive branch. Nevertheless, he appointed Bush to lead the newly created Research and Development Board which took over the duties of the OSRD. Finally, in 1950, President Truman signed the National Science Foundation Act, which was organized along the lines proposed by Bush is his 1945 report, *Science – The Endless Frontier*.[2]

Bush's idea for the NSF was that there needed to be more generous and long-term federal funding of science in colleges, universities, and research centers. He proposed five fundamental principles for the agency:

– there must be stability of funds over a period of years so that long-range programs may be undertaken.
– The agency to administer such funds should be composed of citizens selected only on the basis of their interest in and capacity to promote the work of the agency. They should be persons of broad interest in and understanding of the peculiarities of scientific research and education.
– The agency should promote research through contracts or grants to organizations outside the Federal Government. It should not operate any laboratories of its own.
– Support of basic research in the public and private colleges, universities, and research institutes must leave the internal control of policy, personnel, and the method and scope of the research to the institutions themselves.
– While assuring complete independence and freedom for the nature, scope, and methodology of research carried on in the institutions receiving public funds, and while retaining discretion in the allocation of funds among such institutions, the Foundation proposed herein must be responsible to the President and the Congress.[3]

Bush's intent was clearly to keep civilian research separate from military research (he is quite explicit about this throughout the report). He wanted all NSF employees and contractors to be civilians with scientific backgrounds and did not want the NSF to operate its own laboratories. He wanted to assure that government funding to colleges and universities did not come with any undue governmental influence. The fifth fundamental principle addressed President Truman's concern about accountability.

Although not specified in Bush's proposals, NSF grant proposals were sent out for "peer review" by program officers.[4] The initial low funding levels and the inevitable concentration of grants in elite colleges and universities made the NSF vulnerable to attacks of elitism by members of Congress. A division of labor between the National Institutes of Health and the NSF resulted in the former handling the majority of grants for the health sciences and medicine, and the later dealing only with basic biological research along with research in the other natural sciences. Support for the social sciences was initially low and controversial, but rose gradually.[5]

The significance of this tradition lies in the overwhelming importance of public funding of university research in the United States by the NSF and the NIH primarily. Universities ask for and receive "indirect costs"[6] for each grant awarded to affiliated "principal investigators." An indirect cost is cost that cannot be specifically attributed to an individual project, but which is incurred as a result of the need to provide facilities or administration associated with the grant. An award for biological research, for example, will pay direct costs such as the salaries of researchers and equipment needed to conduct the research, but also indirect costs to the university that supplies the physical and administrative infrastructure for the research.

Many universities depend heavily on indirect costs from "sponsored research." A recent example can be found in the budget for the University of California at Santa Cruz for the 2007-2008 fiscal years.[7]

Figure 1: Where the Funds Come From...

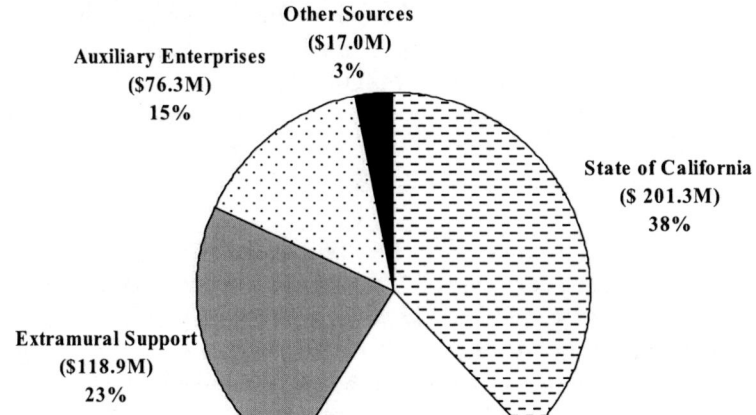

Extramural support includes federal grants made to UCSC researchers, which in this case constituted over 20 % of annual revenues. This was not atypical for research-oriented universities in the United States. My own university, Indiana University, depended about equally on state subsidies and tuition for about half of its revenues. Some states were more generous than others. Some universities, like Johns Hopkins University in Baltimore, were more dependent than UCSC or Indiana on sponsored research. In fiscal year 2006, Johns Hopkins received $1.3 billion in research funding from the NSF, the NIH, the National Aeronautics and Space Agency (NASA), and the Department of Defense (among others), giving it the distinction of being first in the nation in federal funding for the 28th consecutive year.[8]

The National Science Foundation publishes annual rankings of universities in terms of total federally funded research.[9] The University of Washington at Seattle is a far second to Johns Hopkins, followed the University of Michigan, and Stanford University.

Table 1:

Rank	Institution	1999	2000	2001	2002	2003	2004	2005	2006
	Federally financed R&D expenditures at universities and colleges, ranked by FY 2006 expenditures: FY 1999-2006 (Dollars in thousands)								
	All institutions	16,103,436	17,538,286	19,233,421	21,863,925	24,758,853	27,630,624	29,191,369	30,033,156
1	Johns Hopkins U, The	770,580	793,266	879,741	1,022,510	1,106,971	1,229,426	1,277,292	1,307,453
2	U. WA	368,112	389,622	435,103	487,059	565,602	625,218	606,317	650,394
3	U. MI all campuses	334,226	364,033	396,117	444,255	516,818	521,339	554,516	565,739
4	Stanford U.	353,947	367,083	384,468	426,620	483,540	541,667	574,675	540,069
5	U. WI Madison	249,212	278,629	304,009	345,003	396,231	434,423	477,582	491,810
6	U. CA, Los Angeles	251,999	274,162	312,858	366,762	421,174	461,145	469,889	483,873
7	U. PA	279,013	312,434	351,996	397,587	415,631	435,343	465,284	478,773
8	MA Institute of Technology	308,921	306,668	304,319	330,409	356,206	427,552	457,235	476,362
9	U. CA, San Francisco	233,181	248,878	277,489	327,393	371,697	418,944	438,988	464,660
10	U. CA, San Diego	292,007	326,037	343,276	359,383	400,100	465,629	463,946	463,807

Federally financed R & D expenditures at universities and colleges, ranked by FY 2006 expenditures: FY 1999-2006 (Dollars in thousands)

The desire to emulate the success of these universities is a strong motivator for university administrators. Anything that results in increases in federal funding of research is highly valued not just for purposes of prestige but also because of the impact on university revenues. As a result, many universities provide incentives and rewards for faculty that apply successfully for federal grants. This includes giving credit for grant seeking activity in tenure and promotion decisions.

Because success in obtaining grants depends at least partly on scholarly productivity, universities also reward productivity. They might do so in any case, but the need to compete with other universities for federal funding makes it even more desirable. Scholarly productivity is measured, albeit imperfectly in terms of quantity of publications and quality of outlets. Because some book publishers and journals are more prestigious than others, publications of books by prestige presses and journals count more than other publications for tenure and promotion.

Another consequence of the Vannevar Bush approach to federal funding is the stress on basic as opposed to applied research, especially in the sciences. While Bush spoke about the practical implications of research for commerce and the need for universities to maintain control over the intellectual property (patents and copyrights) that resulted from university research, Bush and subsequent policy makers stressed the importance of supporting basic research because they assumed that private firms and laboratories would not be as willing to engage in basic research because it made more sense for private firms to do applied rather than basic research. Applied research was more likely than basic research to result in new products and processes that could affect the corporate bottom line. University researchers would be at a disadvantage because they were too far from the market to understand its imperatives.

Scholars like Edwin Mansfield argued that basic research in universities eventually resulted in new products/processes in any case, so the key to a positive economic impact of university research on the economy was to make sure that there was an efficient way of transferring scientific results and technologies from the university to private sector.[10] This and the desire to control intellectual property made possible by university research led universities to establish bureaus of technology transfer. At Indiana University, the success of Crest fluoride toothpaste became a model for how to manage technology transfer, much to the chagrin of scientists in recent decades.

The Liberal Arts Tradition

Alongside the Vannevar Bush approach to the administration of university research efforts, a much older tradition, that of the liberal arts, remained influential not just for the arts and humanities but also for other disciplines. Many of the university's researchers completed their undergraduate studies at liberal arts colleges where the stress was on a balanced education in a wide variety of disciplines to produce graduates who could transcend disciplinary boundaries and draw upon the best ideas not just to inform their research but to enable them to provide an education to their students that was not overly specialized, and that improved the quality of their lives.

The liberal arts tradition has its routes in Greek and Roman ideas of education.

After Greek philosophy had reached full flower in the fourth century B.C., scholars and teachers sought to establish a curriculum to prepare students for the higher and more difficult studies. Out of these efforts came what was called the *enkuklios paideia*, the learning circle, from which we get our word encyclopedia.

A first century B.C. scholar and statesman named Marcus Terentius Varro codified this slowly developing curriculum into nine disciplines and introduced it to Rome. His work provided a model for Latin scholars ("encyclopedists") of the later Roman period; such famous names as St. Augustine, Boethius, and Cassiodorus refined and developed the tradition; and by the fifth to sixth century A.D. a canon of seven liberal arts (dropping Varro's architecture and medicine) had been established and incorporated into Christian education.

These seven arts were divided into the two familiar categories: the trivium, consisting of the verbal arts of logic, grammar, and rhetoric; and the quadrivium, consisting of the numerical arts of mathematics, geometry, music, and astronomy. These disciplines came to constitute the liberal arts, which "provided the basic content and form of intellectual life [in Europe] for several centuries." The liberal arts were, in effect, regarded as "the seven pillars of wisdom."[11]

The basic idea behind the liberal tradition, therefore, is that all learning must be built on a foundation that requires students and scholars to understand how to use language, logic, mathematics, and other types of puzzle-posing and puzzle-solving tools to advance the state of knowledge. As a result, liberal arts colleges and universities establish distribution requirements for all students who attend so that they will be exposed at least to all these approaches. Regardless of where in the universe of disciplines a given individual decides to invest their time and energy, there is a strong benefit, according to defenders of the liberal arts tradition, for everyone to have this common foundation of learning.

In some respects, the liberal arts tradition is antithetical to the Vannevar Bush approach. Those concerned with maximizing federal grants, for example, to the natural sciences, may find the demands imposed on university resources by advocates of the liberal arts tradition to be inefficient and wasteful. Since many of the disciplines that are supposed to be part of the liberal arts curriculum do not receive any form of federal funding, they may be seen as a drag on the rest of the university's ability to achieve its most important goals (i.e. more government-funded research).

Advocates of the Vannevar Bush approach and the liberal arts tradition share certain values, including, among others, the pursuit of high-quality scholarship as evidenced in publications in visible outlets, the need for students to be educated broadly so that they will be aware of developments in fields or disciplines that are not their main focus but that are still potentially important. For example, no physicist would be unhappy about requiring students to study mathematics or statistics and they might even by willing to encourage them to study philosophy or the history of religion to the extent that great physicists in history have been influenced by these disciplines. Similarly, scholars of comparative literature might want their students to have an exposure to the sciences in order to understand allusions to scientific ideas and discoveries in literature.

Interestingly, the two traditions tend to share a lack of interest in applied scientific and technological research because this area of inquiry is seen as not contributing to the prestige of the university and may drag the university into relationships with governments or private business enterprises that compromise the intellectual independence of universities. Classicists and biologists sometimes agree, therefore, that universities should resist pressures to contribute to economic development through cooperative scientific and technological endeavors with businesses and/or governments.

Transcending the Two Traditions?

Major research universities like Johns Hopkins, Stanford, MIT, and the University of California system have engaged extensively in activities that cross the line that some advocates of the two traditions would like to impose on applied research. A wide variety of institutional innovations have arisen to deal with the concerns of humanists and scientists about the potential loss of intellectual autonomy that might result from these endeavors. These include the creation of special laboratories with contractual relationships with public or private donors, business incubators to allow academics to make the transition from teaching and research to participating in entrepreneurial startups, and special mechanisms to allow some intellectual property rights resulting from government-funded university research to be transferred to startup firms.

It is common for administrations of top research universities to organize "dog and pony shows" to brief government officials and potential investors on university research that might have commercial implications. These special events become a form of university-business-government networking that, in principle, can shorten the time between the creation of new knowledge in the academy and the commercialization of products and services based on that new knowledge. In the so-called "competition state" that has succeeded the "welfare state" in an increasingly globalized world economy, there has been a marked rise in the perceived value of these sorts of university activities. To the extent that this is seen as undermining the purity of both the Vannevar Bush approach and the liberal arts tradition, university faculty invested in those two traditions will continue to resist it.

Endnotes

[1] Joanne Martin, *Organizational Culture: Mapping the Terrain* (Thousand Oaks, Calif.: Sage, 2001); Edgar Schein, "Organizational Culture and Leadership," in Jay Chafitz and J. Steven Ott, eds., Classics *of Organization Theory* (Fort Worth: Harcourt, 2001); Edgar Schein, *Organizational Culture and Leadership,* 3rd Edition (San Francisco: Jossey-Bass, 2004).

[2] G. Pascall Zachary, *Endless Frontier: Vannevar Bush, Engineer of the American Century* (Cambridge, Mass.: MIT Press, 1999).

[3] Vannevar Bush, *Science – The Endless Frontier*, <http://www.nsf.gov/about/history/vbush1945.htm#ch6.3>.

[4] Peer review is an institution considerably older than the National Science Foundation and dates back to the 18th century according to Dale J. Benos et al.: "The Ups and Downs of Peer Review", *Advances in Physiology Education*, Vol. 31 (2007), pp. 145–152. For an argument that peer review had much earlier origins see Ray Spier, "The history of the peer-review process", *Trends in Biotechnology*, Vol. 20 (2002), p. 357-358.

[5] NSF 88-16, *A Brief History* (Washington, D.C.: NSF, July 15, 1994), <http://www.nsf.gov/pubs/stis1994/nsf8816/nsf8816.txt>.

[6] The current formal name is Facilities and Administrative (F&A) costs.

[7] <http://planning.ucsc.edu/budget/reports/profile2007.pdf>.

[8] "Johns Hopkins First in R&D Expenditures for 28th Year," Headlines@Hopklins news release, December 3, 2007, <http://www.jhu.edu/~news_info/news/univ07/dec07/r&d.html>.

[9] <http://www.nsf.gov/statistics/nsf08300/pdf/tab28.pdf>.

[10] See, for example, Edwin Mansfield, "Contribution of R&D to Economic Growth in the United States," *Science*, Vol. 175, No. 4021 (February 4, 1972), 477-486.

[11] Christopher Flannery, "Liberal Arts and Liberal Education," *On Principle*, Vol. 6, No. 3, (June 1998), <http://www.ashbrook.org/publicat/onprin/v6n3/flannery.html>; quotations from David L. Wagner, ed., *The Seven Liberal Arts in the Middle Ages* (Bloomington, Indiana University Press, 1983).

11

Globalization, Competitiveness, and Their Impact on the Changing Nature of Universities in Europe and the U.S.

Ken Gros Louis

I begin with a quote from the book, *"College Learning for the New Global Century"*,[1] published several months ago.

"In recent years, the ground has shifted for Americans in virtually every important sphere of life-economic, global, cross-cultural, environmental, civic. The world around us is being dramatically reshaped by scientific and technological innovations, global interdependence, cross-cultural encounters, and changes in the balance of economic and political power. Only a few years ago, Americans envisioned a future in which this nation would be the only world's superpower. Today it is clear that the United States – and individual Americans – will be challenged to engage in unprecedented ways with the global community, collaboratively and competitively."

Whether you were in attendance at my welcome yesterday or not, let me assure you that IU (Indiana University) is very strong in international areas, including the number of international students, faculty, and study abroad programs. Still, the global context in which we are now operating requires us to change the ways in which the university engages internationally.

The dissolution of the Soviet Union in the early 1990s, economic reforms in China and the emergence of powerful new economies in Japan, India and Korea, brought fundamental changes in the pattern of interaction between these countries and the United States. At the same time IU and other universities began to see an increase in enrollments of students from many of these countries. It seems quite clear to us that if we do not actively engage in strategically focused international teaching and research, we run the risk of being marginalized.

An international strategy for American universities must consist of four components:
– education and service learning abroad;
– global institutional engagement;
– global faculty research; and
– international outreach and service.

Meeting the goals of these components will mean:
– the recruitment of highly qualified international students;
– a new emphasis on expanding student involvement in overseas study Programs especially in the industrialized countries of East and South Asia;
– developing new, strategic partnerships with major institutions of higher education abroad;
– developing the curriculum and introducing an international dimension into undergraduate degree requirements so as to build the global competency of undergraduates;
– providing opportunities for international professional development for faculty as well as recruiting highly qualified international specialists and international faculty;
– expanding international development and fundraising as well as outreach and service.

There are challenges both in the components and in the list I have just enumerated. A number of factors, for example, are affecting the ability in the United States to recruit highly qualified international students – these include the after effects of 9/11; increasing costs of U.S. higher education; increasing competition for international students from other host nations; improved educational quality and capacity of educational systems in many parts of the world; and the perception that visas to the U.S. are difficult to obtain. In fact, these factors have diminished this country's share of international students by approximately 10 % during the past 10 years.

Perhaps the most important thing we in America need to undertake is the development of a comprehensive international student enrollment management strategy. This must include alumni clubs, admissions, international services, and various schools and departments. In concert with this, we must increase financial aid resources to highly qualified international students to enhance our position in the world-wide competition for the best students.

Thus, here in Bloomington, our deans recognized the importance of actively recruiting overseas. We always had staff in the admissions office who handled international applications. But we realized as the competition increased internationally, we needed to ramp up our recruitment activities; in particular, we needed to travel, to advertise – no longer could we be successful by being very good at passively encouraging students to attend IU, we now needed to go out and get them. Funding was put aside to develop informational publications directly aimed at prospective international students, we increased advertising in international university guides, we hired a full-time international recruitment representative. That recruiter travels the world to present information about Indiana University to prospective students. Last year the recruiter visited 12 countries in as many months, including several cities in India, Taiwan, Hong Kong, China, South Korea, and Japan. The effort has certainly proven successful as indicated by the increase in international undergraduate applications by 60 % and graduate applications by 22 % over the course of the past two years. Clearly, we need to continue this aggressive international recruiting effort.

At the same time we hope to increase the rate of participation of our own students in study abroad by 25 % over the next five years.

While we already have more than 200 formal exchange agreements which have served the university well, we must now seek new opportunities for institutional relationships to expand research and exchange activities including the possibility of special consortial arrangements. In the future, it will be necessary to increase investments in faculty international professional development and to recruit on a worldwide basis. Last year, 12.5 % of our faculty in Bloomington came from other countries; we expect to double that number over the next five years.

As we have become involved with universities in other countries, doing collaborative research and exchanges, we have focused on six areas: the environment; global health issues; economic development; terrorism and national security; education and literacy; and building democratic societies. Other universities certainly have other and different priorities.

And yet as we plan, knowing that our peers across the country are also involved in similar planning, a number of questions arise for all of us.[2] For example, are overseas summer internships, semester long exchanges or course based study trips more effective in terms of student learning and engagement? How should faculty in various schools and disciplines go about determining which type of international component is more effective? Indeed it may be the case that these will differ from school to school.

Similarly, faculty will want to know what provisions are being made to provide support for their greater emphasis on international and global issues in their teaching, scholarship, and service. Students will want to know what benefits will accrue to them from increased attention to international and global content in their academic programs. Citizens in every state will want to know how expanding international activity will enhance the economic and cultural vitality of the state.

Even more basic questions – does the term "campus" hold the same meaning now as it did before the telecommunications revolution enabled scholars to share the products of their creativity across continents and cultures? Has the world's precarious political climate resulted in a need to be more cautious when universities open their doors to the world? What implications might this have for student and faculty exchanges?

This campus and others have a long history of providing international service, frequently at the request of the federal government and other funders. Given these successes and future needs, how will universities allocate resources to future international projects and initiatives? What process will be used to establish priorities for international work? What criteria will be used to make decisions about international priorities, strategic directions, and international partners? Can a university's decision in this area be based on short or medium term needs and objectives which have a longer term set of goals and priorities articulated? What are the appropriate timeframes for such planning initiatives?

Along with the answer to the question of partnerships, is the issue of the location of those partners. With a long standing tradition of research and development work around the world, should a university direct a significant portion of its resources to a particular world region? And will a focus on a particular region at the expense of others limit the university's potential to carry out important work in other world regions which provide opportunities that may not offer immediate high rates of return to the university?

We already teach a large number of languages. The post 9/11 political climate has raised the question of the need to improve the teaching of "strategic languages" that can assist national security in the United States. But what of languages that are not considered to be strategic but are nonetheless critical for understanding world cultures? How can universities avoid making decisions about which languages to teach based solely on current strategic interests at the expense of other priorities, such as the preservation of threatened indigenous cultures?

Obviously, we all need to do a great deal of work to internationalize the curriculum. But what will the effect of that be on students? What additional coursework that deals with global and international issues will broaden their perspectives on current challenges facing the world? Will they become global citizens? Will they opt for other international educational activities and opportunities? How should we balance future investments in international general education against more specialized disciplinary strengths? As undergraduate demands for Chinese and Spanish increase, for example, will offerings in Mongolian and Catalan be scaled back? In some ways the challenge of the undergraduate curriculum re-emphasizes the stress of the globalization process more than research or service. To what extent are students' experiences likely to become homogenized through efforts to coordinate and plan centrally? We need to encourage and support multiple forms of assessment that will capture the nature of the study abroad experience and its impact on students.

For public universities, we must continue to grapple with the tension between the moral obligations to provide quality teaching, research, and service to students and community and the push to become an institution that promotes economic growth. How can we identify the most critical problems, provide needed assistance and ensure sustainability of efforts, and at the same time maintain our core values as public universities with a responsibility to the welfare of the citizens of each state?

There are certainly challenges ahead of us. As we ponder the connection between where American universities have been and where they are going with their global and international work, a dialogue to address these and other questions raised here could provide valuable insights into the choices that are to be made and their implications for the short and long term future of international activity in the United States.

Endnotes

[1] *College Learning for the New Global Century,* Association of American College and Universities, Washington, D.C. 2007.

[2] This and several of the following observations are based, in part on the distillation of ideas expressed by faculty and administrators, reported as part of the Indiana University Bloomington campus reaccreditation Higher Learning Commission self study document.

12

Strategies to Meet the Challenges Facing Tertiary Education Systems

Arthur M. Hauptman

Policy makers around the world face an insistent and consistent set of challenges in plotting the future course of their tertiary education systems. Chief among these are:
- ensuring that the combination of public and private resources available to fund tertiary education is sufficient to keep up with the rapidly growing demand for more education and training among a broad range of the population;
- improving equity throughout the educational pipeline so that groups of students who traditionally have been underserved are ready to do college level work, have access to a suitable program and succeed in sufficient numbers to receive degrees;
- increasing the external efficiency of the system by ensuring tertiary education programs are of sufficient quality and relevant to emerging societal and economic needs of the population, including having a work force capable of allowing for full competition in a global economy
- raising the internal efficiency of the tertiary system by improving productivity through reining in the growth of spending per student and ensuring that students complete their educational programs within a reasonable amount of time.

This brief essay describes some of the strategies that various countries have used to meet these four related challenges in the past and speculates on what they might do in the future. The following table summarizes the range of possible responses that are described in greater detail below.

Challenges	Some Strategies and Policy Responses			
Expand Resources to Match Demand: Models of Growth	Increase public funding to allow for expansion of public institutions	Publicly-financed fees introduced to be repaid as % of income once students graduate	Expand privately- paid tuition fees in public insts w/ more student aid	Create or expand private insts to meet increased demand
Examples	U.S. – in 50s&60s; some Scandinavian countries in 80s&90s	Australia (1988); England (2006); Thailand (2006)	New Zealand in 90s; Canada; U.S. 80s&90s	# of Asian and Middle Eastern countries; Poland
Improve Equity for Student Readiness, Access & Success	Tuition fees at public insts set well below cost of education	Institutions are paid more for the low-income students they enroll/graduate	Grants reduce the need to borrow by low-income and/ or high-merit students	Students in public& private insts borrow for fees &/or living costs
Examples	Most countries	England, Ireland	U.S.; Canada; NZ	Several dozen countries
Ensure High Quality & Relevance (External Efficiency)	Institutions must meet minimal standards to qualify for public funding	Funding formulas pay institutions more for courses deemed most relevant	Competitive funds are used to stimulate quality, relevance, and innovation	Grants provided or loans forgiven for students enrolled in relevant studies
Examples		England	> dozen countries	U.S. loan forgiveness
Increase Productivity (Internal Efficiency)	Performance-based funding provisions are implemented	A higher % of public funds are allocated to sectors of lower-cost institutions	Allocations of public funds based on average or normative costs per student	Market forces make insts become more competitive and productive
Examples	England, Denmark; France, US states	California Master Plan – 1950s&60s	Czech Republic; other East. Europe countries	

Challenge One: Matching Resources to Keep Up with Rapidly Growing Demand

Over the past half century, more than a dozen countries around the world have employed a variety of strategies to move from traditional elite systems of tertiary education to mass or universal ones in which at least a majority of the traditional college-age population enrolls in tertiary education. Understanding which strategies were employed is useful in assessing how these and other countries in the future may be able to manage to keep up with a burgeoning demand for tertiary education that comes largely from the increasing economic returns associated with additional education and training beyond the secondary school level. A review of the strategies employed suggests four models of growth:

Rapid Expansion of a Public Sector Charging Little or no Tuition Fees

This is perhaps the most prevalent model of growth over the past half century. Countries make a financial commitment of public funds sufficient to expand their public sectors of tertiary education without requiring large or even significant cost sharing in the form of higher fees from students and families. One reasonable definition of this approach would be that tuition fees represent 10 percent or less of the resources used to pay for instructional and operational expenses (excluding research and other activities). The U.S. in the 1950s and 1960s would be an example of a country that employed such a strategy to move to a mass education system beyond the secondary level. This included the development of a thousand community colleges and the creation and expansion of hundreds of four year public institutions. In the past quarter century, this strategy also has been used by at least several Scandinavian countries including Norway, Sweden, and Finland.

The critical component for successful implementation of this strategy is a country's willingness and ability to devote substantial levels of public resources (in excess of 1.5 percent of GDP) to allow for expansion without requiring significant levels of cost sharing. In reality, most countries today are not in a position to make this kind of commitment of public funding.

Publicly Financed Fees Repaid Through the Tax System Once Students Graduate

Australia established a new model for growth in the late 1980s when it introduced its Higher Education Contribution Scheme (HECS). The impetus for this strategy was recognition of two realities. First, there was the financial reality that private resources were needed to supplement public resources to fuel needed growth of higher education. Second, there was the political reality that most students and their families were unwilling to pay traditional fees. Dealing with these realities, Australia developed an approach in which the government would initially finance fees, with most of these students repaying the fees once they graduated as a percentage of their income through the income tax system. England has introduced a similar system of publicly financed fees beginning in the academic year 2006. Thailand also has adopted a similar system.

A key question with regard to publicly financed fees, like the model of public sector expansion, is whether a country has enough resources to fund it. Under this approach, governments essentially are funding both sides of the tertiary financing equation – operational support of institutions and the payment of fees by students and families – until the stream of loan repayments is sufficient to provide significant private resources. Even a country as wealthy as Australia has found that it needed to reduce subsidies in HECS by lowering the incomes that qualify for non-repayment and raising the HECS fees to make the system sustainable. In addition, many Australian institutional officials would claim that public support of institutions has been reduced to make ends meet.

*Increased Cost Sharing, Usually Combined With Higher Levels
of Student Aid*

A third model of growth is one in which more significant cost recovery through higher fees is introduced at a wide range of public institutions. This is usually combined with greater reliance on student aid to ensure that economically disadvantaged students are not discouraged from attending by the higher fees being charged. Countries using this approach to expand resources to meet rapidly growing demand include the U.S. over the past quarter century, New Zealand in the 1990s, and Canada for the past two decades.

Although raising fees for all public sector students is typically thought of as the basic policy response for greater cost sharing, the reality is that there are a number of different ways in which countries raise fees to increase their degree of cost sharing. In many Eastern European countries, a system of parallel fees has been established in which students who do not qualify for the "free seats" based on grades and merit can enroll in the same courses of study by paying tuition fees that are set at or near the full cost of education. This is not recommended as it introduces or reinforces system inequities.

But there are other ways in which fees can be raised selectively which make a great deal of sense for spurring growth and introducing greater equity. These include:

A dual system of fees:

A number of countries are moving in the direction of a dual system in which highly subsidized fees are applied to students in state-funded places, while higher "market-based" fees equal or close to full costs are charged in high demand fields such as business or law. (This is not the same as parallel fees in which students taking the same courses pay sharply different amounts of fees.) Australia is a prime example of a country that has moved to a dual fee structure in which students in its HECS system pay (or repay through loans) according to government set fees, whereas all foreign students and a small but growing number of domestic students pay at much higher rates. A growing number of other countries now charge more for market-based programs than the regular course of study. Many European countries utilize a system of dual fees for students from non-EU countries. A dual system of fees could also be based on the social relevance and priority of different fields of study.

Differential fees by level of study:

It is a common practice in many countries to have fee structures in which groups of students pay different levels of fees: very low or no fees for undergraduates; higher fees for graduate students, international students, and in some instances adult learners. Ireland is a good example of a country that does not charge tuition fees for undergraduates (the government pays these fees), but that charges fees for other groups of students including adult learners and those enrolled in graduate programs. In many if not most countries, graduate students are charged more than undergraduates.

Expansion of a Private Sector of Institutions

A fourth model of growth is one in which enrollments in private institutions expand to take up the slack created from restrictions in the size and growth of the public sector of tertiary education. This has occurred in a number of countries around the world either as a matter of deliberate government strategies or simply as an example of an industry developing in response to unmet demand. In the Middle East and some countries in Asia, the number of private sector institutions and students has grown particularly in vocational programs, although private universities have been the primary source of growth in some countries such as Japan and Korea. Poland is an example of an Eastern European country that has become a mass higher education system largely as a result of the growth of a private sector.

In some cases, the private institutions are for-profit while in others their organization is typically not-for-profit, with surpluses reinvested in the institution. What is common, though, is that most of the enrolment growth in these countries occurs in the private sector while the number of students enrolling in public sector institutions remain stable or grow very slowly as additional public funds are not made available. One way to encourage more enrolment in the private sector is to make students enrolling in these institutions eligible for the full range of student financial assistance and student loans with the government taking responsibility for ensuring institutions meet minimal academic and financial standards to avoid market abuses.

Challenge Two: Improving Equity Throughout the Educational Pipeline

Improving equity – by providing greater access for economically disadvantaged students and other traditionally underserved groups of students - has become a central policy concern in many countries around the world over the past quarter century. In discussing access and equity as a fundamental policy concern, it is important to distinguish between overall access issues as discussed above, and equity concerns about the gaps in participation and persistence among different groups of students. Increasing access technically pertains to increasing the overall participation rate in tertiary education although concerns about equity are often included in debates on the subject.

Most of the models for growth described in the section above often do not place equity high on the agenda, unless they employ an aggressive system of non-repayable student financial aid or income contingent student loan repayment that is made available to a significant proportion of the student population. Thus, the pressure increases in both high growth and low growth situations to ensure that traditionally disadvantaged groups of students have more adequate access to tertiary education.

Typically, strong support is expressed at least rhetorically for the need to improve equity of access to tertiary education systems. The reality, however, is that few countries have made significant strides in closing equity gaps or in having systems that achieve a high degree of equity. The few countries or states/provinces that can make this claim generally have a high degree of homogeneity in their populations that permit greater equity in tertiary education as well as many other societal functions. A corollary to this is that equity in access becomes more difficult to achieve as immigration levels increase.

A number of strategies might be or have been used to achieve greater equity, including:

Require Institutions to Enroll More Low-Income Students

The most direct way to achieve greater equity is for governments to require institutions to enroll certain numbers of targeted groups of students in order to receive public funding. In many ways this is not so much a funding issue as a regulatory matter. Few if any countries have taken this approach, as it would be viewed in most countries as an unreasonable intrusion by government on institutional autonomy to require institutions to enroll certain students. A more likely scenario would be for government bodies in charge of quality review and assurance processes or NGOs such as accrediting bodies to include equity and access considerations in their review and approval of institutions and programs.

Subsidize Tuition Fees at Public Institutions

The most frequent strategy around the world for increasing access and equity has been for governments to provide enough operating support to public institutions that allow them to hold tuition fees well below the cost of providing that education. This policy is based on an obvious premise: that the most direct way to promote greater equity is to keep prices low, thereby spurring greater demand. Policy makers in most countries subscribe to this theory.

The reality, however, is that low tuition fees at public institutions is a rather inequitable policy for at least two reasons. One is that under a system where fees are set well below cost, the public subsidies go to all students enrolled in those institutions, rich and poor alike. To the extent that students are admitted on the basis of merit and highly correlated with high socioeconomic status, public subsidies tend to be distributed regressively.

It is also important to recognize that tuition fees are an important part of both demand and supply of tertiary education. The typical emphasis on keeping tuition fees low is tied to the notion that lower prices will spur demand. But fees also represent one of the primary sources of revenues for instruction and operations; keeping tuition fees low means that fewer seats can be provided for any given level of public support. This is another reason that low tuition often does not result in greater access and equity in many countries.

Pay Institutions More For the Low-Income Students They Enroll and Graduate

In most countries, equity concerns are typically addressed through student financial aid and other student-based policies. But a few countries are beginning to recognize the importance of affecting institutional behavior in trying to achieve higher degree of equity at different points on the educational pipeline. England was one of the first countries to move in this direction by establishing a low-income student "premium" in its funding process in which institutions are paid more for students who reside in postal codes with high concentrations of low-income students. Ireland has followed suit by setting up a similar provision in its funding system. But these are exceptions rather than the rule.

Institutional incentives need not be limited to enrolling more low-income and other disadvantaged groups of students. To the extent that equity concerns typically extend to the chronically low numbers of economically disadvantaged students who graduate from the programs in which they enroll, incentives also might be used to encourage institutions to graduate more of these students. This is an example of "payments for results" discussed at greater length in the section on performance-based funding options.

Provide More Non-Repayable Aid

Providing grants, scholarships, and other forms of non-repayable aid is perhaps the most prevalent policy for enhancing equity in countries around the world. This aid takes many forms and is provided based on various rules of eligibility. To improve equity of access, the aid should be conditioned on students demonstrating a measure of financial need. While most non-repayable aid is need-based, in many countries eligibility for scholarships is merit-based or a combination of need and merit. The administrative structures for providing grants also widely vary, but typically take one of two basic forms: Govern-ment-provided aid and institutional discounts.

Government Aid Programs

In most countries, governmental units fund programs that provide aid to tertiary students to cover some combination of their tuition fees and living expenses. Eligibility for this aid typically is determined through government rules although institutional officials may well be responsible for administering these programs. Vouchers would be an alternative administrative structure in which aid would be distributed based on which institutions student recipients choose to attend.

Institutional Discounts

Another approach for providing aid is for institutions to raise their tuition and other fees to generate more resources and then use some of these funds to provide discounts to reduce the price that certain groups of students actually pay. The U.S. experience over the past quarter century is particularly instructive. It began in the late 1970s as a few elite private institutions decided that they were underpriced relative to their economic value; they aggressively began to raise their prices while simultaneously increasing their student aid budgets. The success of this "high tuition/high aid" strategy at these few institutions led a number of other private institutions in the 1980s to pursue it. In the 1990s and into the new century, an increasing number of public insti-tutions have adopted this strategy as well, although to a lesser degree than at private institutions. A number of institutions in other countries have utilized this strategy as well – what is essential for this strategy to work, however, is for institutions to have authority to set and retain their tuition fees so they are in a position to discount their prices.

Less mentioned in these discussions is the centrality of student loans to the success of the high tuition/high aid approach. In the U.S., it is difficult to imagine that most institutions would have been able to carry out these high tuition/high aid policies without enough availabil-ity of government-backed student loans. In the past several years, a new twist has been added: some of the best private and public institutions have declared they will provide enough additional grant aid to prevent students from the lowest income families from having to borrow at all. It remains to be seen whether this becomes a larger trend.

Expanded Use of Student Loans

More than fifty countries now have some form of student loan program in place. These programs take a number of forms and have a number of purposes. A principal purpose of having governments getting involved in providing or sponsoring student loans is to correct for market imperfections that otherwise would prevent students from being able to invest in themselves. Another related reason is to permit greater cost sharing in which students and their families pay a higher percentage of the costs of providing tertiary education. But improving the equity of the system – giving students with less family resources a better chance of going to college – underlies all of these loan arrangements.

The international evidence on whether student loans help close chronic equity gaps is mixed. The availability of student loans clearly expands opportunities for a broad range of students and in doing so has the potential for making tertiary systems much more equitable than ones that do not use loans as a financing mechanism. On the other hand, most student loan programs have unacceptable non-repayment rates and introduce administrative requirements that many countries have difficulty handling.

Challenge Three: Ensuring Adequate Quality and Relevance (External Efficiency)

It has long been obvious that improving quality and relevance of tertiary education is critical if countries are to be competitive internationally. Businesses simply are unable to compete on the global stage when countries lack a well-trained work force. The problem is that most countries have not taken the necessary steps to ensure their systems of tertiary education are of high quality and relevant to their society's emerging needs.

Quality and relevance are the two key components of what economists might call the external efficiency of education systems – the degree to which different elements of society are "satisfied" with the students that emerge from the educational system. Most observers would also agree that quality and relevance are linked concepts – a tertiary education system is unlikely to be relevant to society's needs if it is not of high enough quality in its programs, faculty, and students.

But while quality and relevance are linked as key objectives for improving external efficiency and effectiveness, the role of public policy in promoting them is very different between the two. Public policies, particularly as they relate to financing, are quite limited in what they can achieve in improving system quality for several reasons. For one, measures of quality are not easily determined in a way that would be useful for funding formulas or negotiated budgets. It is difficult to promote better quality because it is difficult to measure quality in a systematic way. The reality is that regulatory quality assurance procedures are needed to ensure minimal quality and to promote excellence. Finally, maintaining and improving quality is ultimately an institutional responsibility; the most government can expect to do is to encourage better quality, not produce it.

With these caveats in mind, there are some limited ways in which public policies can have a positive effect on quality:

- among programs of institutional support, competitive funds may be the best for stimulating better quality because they allow for more sophisticated quality assessments than more general funding mechanisms
- merit-based student aid programs can help to promote better preparation and achievement of students and can promote equity as well if the amount of aid provided is also linked in some way to financial need of students
- vouchers may also promote quality by allowing students to choose the best quality programs and institutions. But this assumes a sufficient degree of student mobility within the system, a condition that often is not met.

In contrast to the limited role public policy can play in stimulating better quality, there are a number of ways in which governments can make tertiary systems more relevant. This governmental role in promoting greater relevance applies both to institution-based policies and student-based policies. For example, in the public funding of institutions:

– priority-based funding systems in which institutions are paid more for seats in high priority fields of study are well suited for promoting more relevance;
– competitive funds in which relevance is a key criterion can also be effective in promoting greater relevance;
– relevance can and also should be a key variable in the allocation of research funds although an examination of research policies in many countries suggests this is often not the case.

Relevance also can be promoted through the direct support of students, in a number of ways:

– higher aid awards can be provided to students who enroll in fields of study deemed to be high priority or relevant;
– better loan terms and conditions can be provided for students enrolling in high priority fields of study;
– all or some student debt can be forgiven for borrowers who take jobs in areas of shortage or high priority.

The key for both institution-based and student-based policies is to have a good system for identifying high priority fields of study and areas of employment. This is no small task, as identifying and projecting areas of high societal or economic need can be a very tricky business. Shortages today can become surpluses tomorrow, and vice versa.

Challenge Four: Increasing Productivity
(Improving Internal Efficiency)

A key element for tertiary systems to match resources with growing demand is to become more productive, to increase their internal efficiency in various ways such as moderating costs or increasing throughput in the form of greater degree completion. The most obvi-

ous means for improving productivity is to make systems more performance-based. Another is to use public policies to moderate the cost
structure of the tertiary system by using the funding systems to reward
more efficient and productive institutions as measured by their costs
per student or costs per graduate. A third approach would rely on
market mechanisms to create an environment that encourages greater
productivity.

Institute Performance-Based Funding Mechanisms

Internationally, one of the more notable recent trends in tertiary
education is the increased experimentation and reliance on performance-based funding mechanisms. These mechanisms are distinguished
from more traditional allocation processes in that they use measures of
performance as the primary criteria for funding rather than using inputs such as staff costs or participation measures such as the number
of students enrolled. Four types of performance-based mechanisms to
consider are:

–   performance set asides – a portion of public funding for tertiary
    education is set aside to pay institutions on the basis of their
    achieving various performance targets. In the 1990s, a dozen states
    in the U.S. set aside a portion of public funds to be distributed on a
    basis of output measures and ratios;
–   performance contracts – governments enter into binding agree-
    ments with institutions, with resource levels linked to achievement
    of mutually determined performance-based objectives. Perform-
    ance contracts have been implemented in France and several states
    in the U.S. including Colorado and Virginia;
–   competitive funds – institutions or faculty compete on the basis of
    peer reviewed project proposals against a set of policy objectives.
    More than a dozen countries have established competitive funds of
    one form of another. These are also discussed in the section on
    improving quality and relevance;
–   payments for results – output or outcome measures are used to de-
    termine all or a portion of distributions from a funding formula, or
    institutions are paid on a contracted basis for the number of stu-
    dents graduating in certain fields of study or with specific skills.

Denmark and England are examples of countries that have implemented payment for results regimes. Denmark allocates a portion of its formula funds based on the number of graduates. England allocates all its formula funds based on the number of students who complete a year of study.

Allocate More Funds to Low-Cost Sectors of Institutions

In addition to performance-based measures, another way to promote greater productivity is to seek ways to reduce costs in the system. Several public policies relating to the allocation of funds to institutions can be used to promote greater efficiency and lower costs. One of these is for government and funding bodies to allocate a higher proportion of funds to institutions with lower costs per student. Economists refer to this as increasing allocative efficiency. It can be best accomplished by shifting funds to those institutions that are more efficient as measured by lower costs per student. The California Master Plan in the 1950s and 1960s is one example of this approach. It allowed the state to take an average level of public support and provide above average amounts of funds to each of its three public sectors – research universities (University of California), state colleges (which have since become the California State University), and the growing number of community colleges.

Using Average or Normative Costs to Allocate Funds to Public Institutions

Most funding formulas and negotiated budgets take the actual cost per student as reported by institutions to be the basis for determining how much funds to allocate to each institution. But this traditional approach presents several potential problems. One is that it relies on institutions to report their costs and enrollments to governmental or funding bodies, a reliance that can lead to substantial data manipulation. A bigger potential problem is that using actual costs per student can encourage individual institutions either to increase their expenses or restrict their enrollments. Thus, policies in place may lead to cost escalation rather than cost moderation.

One way to address this concern is for funding bodies not to use actual costs per student in deciding how funds are to be allocated to institutions. An alternative is to average costs across the system so that no one institution can benefit from being inefficient. A better approach, in the view of at least some observers, is to move to a system of normative costs in which judgments about optimal student/faculty ratios and other measures of efficiency are embedded in the funding formula.

Rely on Market Forces to Stimulate Higher Productivity

Still another approach for achieving greater productivity is for countries to increase their reliance on the private sector to provide tertiary education. After all, in many fields of endeavor, market mechanisms are relied upon to stimulate greater competition among providers. This economic theory as applied to tertiary education would suggest that the laws of supply and demand will force institutions to keep their costs low and their productivity high in order to attract students, staff, and resources as opposed to increasing profits. This approach in tertiary education would mean that public agencies refrain from imposing restrictions on public and private universities to allow their competitive juices to flow.

This notion of relying on the private sector to increase productivity is more theory than practice, however. Few governments have been willing to cede large degrees of autonomy to institutions. Nor does it seem that when institutions are allowed to compete lower costs per student are necessarily the result. If the experience in the U.S. is any guide, allowing institutions to compete for students can lead to higher costs as many institutions seek to attract students through more amenities rather than lower costs.

In sum, tertiary education systems around the world face daunting challenges, made more so by limited resources. How governments or institutions will react to these challenges is difficult to predict. If recent experience is any guide, the past may well not be prologue.

Index

List of Authors

David Audretsch, Distinguished Professor and Ameritech Chair of Economic Development and Director of the Institute for Development Strategies, School of Public and Environmental Affairs, Indiana University, Bloomington, Indiana, USA; Director, Entrepreneurship, Growth and Public Policy, Max Planck Institute of Economics, Jena, Germany

Hans-Jürgen Blinn, Head of the "International and European Affairs" unit of the Ministry of Education, Science, Youth, Culture of Rhineland-Palatinate, Mainz, Germany

Eberhard Bohne, Professor of Public Administration, Policy and Law for Environmental Protection and Energy, German University of Administrative Sciences Speyer, Speyer, Germany

Charles F. Bonser, Dean Emeritus, Indiana University, School of Public and Environmental Affairs, Bloomington, Indiana, USA

Laure Castin, Professor and Head of International Relations, University of Reims Champagne-Ardenne, Reims, France

Ken Gros Louis, University Chancellor of Indiana University, Bloomington, Indiana, USA

Jeffrey A. Hart, Professor, Department of Political Science, Indiana University, Bloomington, Indiana, USA

Arthur M. Hauptman, independent public policy consultant and internationally recognized expert in higher education finance, Arlington, Virginia, USA

Manuel Heitor, Secretary of State for Science, Technology, and Higher Education for the Government of Portugal, Lisbon, Portugal

Michael Kelly, Chairman, Higher Education Authority of Ireland, Dublin, Ireland

Siegfried Magiera, Chair of Public Law and the Jean Monnet Chair of European Law at the German University of Administrative Sciences Speyer, Speyer, Germany

Frans-Bauke van der Meer, Associate Professor of Public Administration concentrating on Public Management, and Director of the part time mid-career MSc program in Public Administration, both at Erasmus University Rotterdam, The Netherlands

Arthur Ringeling, Professor of Public Administration, concentrating on problems of Administration and Policy, Erasmus University Rotterdam, Rotterdam, The Netherlands

Alan M. Rugman, Professor of International Business, Professor of Business Economics and Public Policy, and the L. Leslie Waters Chair of International Business, Kelley School of Business, Indiana University, Bloomington, Indiana USA